The Done Thing

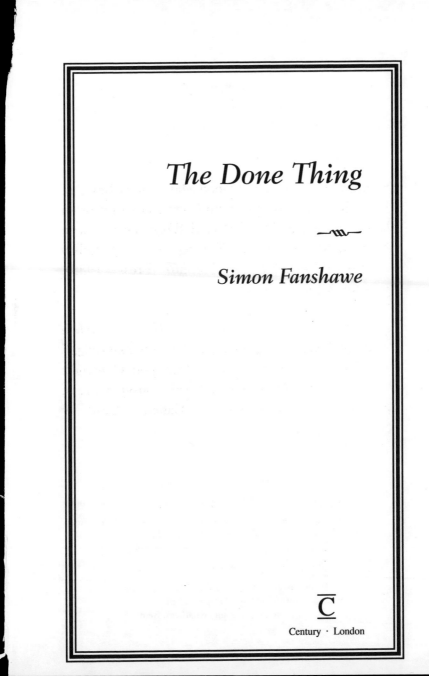

The Done Thing

—⁓—

Simon Fanshawe

Century · London

Published by Century in 2005

1 3 5 7 9 10 8 6 4 2

Copyright © Simon Fanshawe 2005

Simon Fanshawe has asserted his right under the Copyright, Designs and
Patents Act 1988 to be identified as the author of this work

Every effort has been made to contact all original copyright holders.
The publisher will be happy to make any necessary corrections
to future printings

First published in the United Kingdom in 2005 by Century
The Random House Group Limited
20 Vauxhall Bridge Road, London SW1V 2SA

Random House Australia (Pty) Limited
20 Alfred Street, Milsons Point, Sydney,
New South Wales 2061, Australia

Random House New Zealand Limited
18 Poland Road, Glenfield,
Auckland 10, New Zealand

Random House South Africa (Pty) Limited
Endulini, 5a Jubilee Road, Parktown 2193, South Africa

The Random House Group Limited Reg. No. 954009
www.randomhouse.co.uk

A CIP catalogue record for this book is available from the British Library

Papers used by Random House are natural, recyclable products made
from wood grown in sustainable forests. The manufacturing processes
conform to the environmental regulations of the country of origin

ISBN 1 8441 3873 9

Typeset by SX Composing DTP, Rayleigh, Essex
Printed and bound in Great Britain by
Mackays of Chatham plc, Chatham, Kent

CONTENTS

If my mother and father hadn't taught me what they did as I grew up I would never have written this book. If my mother hadn't died two years ago I wouldn't have been able to write it. If my sister and brother, Sarah and Richard, didn't support me with their enthusiasm and love then I wouldn't have done half the things I have been able to. My friends Brenda, Nobby, David, Bryony, Jess, Anna, Andrew, Matt, Mary, Mark, Peter, Russell, Paul, Sandra, Basil, Charlie, Tony, Graeme, Graham (and the lovely couples) Gerard and Paul, Jane and Will, Joy and Jo, Jackie and Mark, Mel and David, Roy and Noreen, all love me I know, and me them, but, boy, have they all been sweet and patient as I have gone on and on about this book. And they have enthused and kept me going.

Penelope Leach was most generous with her time and advice about children. Margaret Visser's research has been irreplaceable. John Mullan, a school friend who has become a distinguished authority on the eighteenth-century kindly introduced me to its delights and importance. If Kate Watkins at Random House hadn't asked me to write a book in the first place, finger would never have been put to keyboard. She has been a brilliant editor, playing me like an instrument to keep me going, make me change things and give me confidence. Nick Ranceford-Hadley is a wise and clever agent.

The Done Thing is dedicated to all these people. To Erasmus, who had a brain the size of the planet and humanity the breadth of the ocean. But it's really dedicated to all those of you who will join this campaign of civil obedience and take it upon yourselves just to be decent to each other and stimulate that in others, whether they are your children, your fellow passengers, pedestrians, drivers or colleagues, your friends, spouses, lovers or just people you pass in the street.

Simon Fanshawe
Brighton
February 2005

—ᄱ—

INTRODUCTION

This is a book about manners. So thank you for reading
it. None of us want to spend the rest of our lives
standing by doors that we've held open muttering to
someone as they sweep through, without so much as a
smile or a thanks, 'Not at all, never mind, no problem.
I love opening doors for people. It's my life's work.' Nor
do we want just to scurry away wondering why we
bothered in the first place. And the reason we hold the
door open, or give up our seat, or write a thank-you
letter – and these are just tiny, tiny specks of
consideration for other people compared with true
grace under the pressure of living – is not because
there is some ferocious schoolmarm in the sky with a
big ruler threatening to rap us over the knuckles for
not being polite. It's because every opened door

ignored, every seat not given up for an older person, every present not acknowledged, every meal without thanks, every mobile phone screamed into that crashes into the peace of others, every puff of smoke blown into somebody else's face is a breaking of the bonds of care that we should feel between one another.

They are small things, but they are symbolic. We open a door to someone or help them with their pram because, even for a moment, we simply want to confirm our social nature, to say that we belong to a world that we all can own and that we are not locked away in a personal bubble ignorant of anyone else. And without overloading door opening or pram carrying with too much significance, nonetheless we want to be thanked, not because we're smug and want to feel that we've been a little goody-two-shoes. Rather more modestly we only want to be acknowledged. With each of these gestures there is much more at stake than just tiny expressions of politeness. When you give a present to someone, to be thanked is simply to confirm the friendship that the present embodied. And if the absence of those simple acknowledgements becomes the accepted norm then self-interest becomes the higher god at whose altar we worship to the exclusion of everybody else. Oh dear. Two paragraphs in and we're already furious. But who really wants to go through life being ignored by selfish people who can't be bothered to think about anybody else, for goodness sake? It chips away at our quality of life and drives us nuts. And not because we are a bunch of old fogeys either.

There is a certain illusion about the past. There always is. It's like the old joke says about the folk singers changing the light bulb. There are always plenty of people to sing about how lovely the old bulb was. But we need to be wary of the nostalgia. Yearning always accompanies change. The boost to those liberated by the energies of the sixties was followed by a sentimental depression, mainly in others, brought on by the subsequent uncertainty. Nostalgia was the result. But, for instance, were cities any easier to live in in the past.

Have you ever seen *Oliver!*? Well, all right have you read Dickens? A hoard of trained pickpockets terrorising the streets of London may be cute on the stage, but they weren't particularly sweet without make-up. In Dickens's novels you find descriptions of city life that confirm just what criminal anarchy there was by day and by night. Nearer to our own time, the crime rate in the 1920s was considerably higher and you only have to read Alexander McArthur and H. Kingsley Long's epic Glasgow novel from the following decade, *No Mean City*, to get a sense of the endemic public and private violence of life at least in that Scottish city. When an older generation is nostalgic about manners it is often thinking about the fifties. And the Second World War had a unique effect on the unity of purpose of the social fabric. There is no doubt about that.

The memories of the older generation are not entirely wistful. There were more rules then, certainly, not just in public but in private. There was a far greater lexicon of etiquette, endless ritualised ways of saying hello and goodbye and how-do-you-do. Social class determined who called whom sir or madam; men wore hats and took them off only for ladies; village folk sat at the back of the church while the lord and lady of the manor sat at the front; children were 'seen and not heard', port was passed to the left and no one smoked before the Queen was toasted. And for children rules were enforced mainly by fear.

While there may have been rules there was also a great deal less freedom. And while the middle classes were gliding through a life apparently blessed by manners, no one was being that polite to black people or the Irish when they put up the notorious sign in Notting Hill, 'No Irish No dogs No Blacks'. No one was being that polite to women in violent marriages who couldn't get a divorce. No one was being that polite to children beaten into submisson by their fathers to enforce rules they may not have understood. No one was being that polite to anyone who didn't have a voice. Manners are not the abstract rules beloved of the etiquette writers; rather they flow from the principles of respect for and ease with each other. Manners are an agreement about ways of behaving to one another that simply makes life more enjoyable and less of an anxiety to live. And we don't want to hark back to the old but rather look forward to making a new one.

In so doing we will need to renegotiate the bargain between individual freedom and the constraints of social rules to suit how we live now. We make a sacrifice either way. If we have complete individual freedom then we will have no manners. But if we can make some agreement about how we exercise restraint on the single-minded pursuit of solely our own desires, if we can practise consideration towards others in pursuit of the general good, then for our loss of freedom we gain more manners and greater ease with each other. This is an argument that looks forward to a new settlement, not back to an old era. It starts from the conviction that, to use a hackneyed but profound old phrase, there is such a thing as society and that manners confirm it. We just have to agree on some modern ones.

This is absolutely not a book of etiquette. It doesn't much care about which way the port is passed round the table. Which, if you are at all interested, is simply a naval pun. It goes to the left. The port gets passed from port to port. If the country had been called Starboard-ugal it would have gone the other way. The direction doesn't matter. What matters is that it goes in only one. Because that way everybody can get equally cockeyed. Sharing food is the hallmark of hospitality and making sure everyone gets an equal crack at the booze is just one way of showing that everybody is equally welcome at the table. And that's as good a metaphor for manners as any. But the trouble with rules like the one about port is that there's only any value in them if everybody knows and shares them. Otherwise they just trip people up.

Manners are the conventions we devise and accept in order to smooth our relationships with each other. They are not designed to change society but to make it easier to live in. They should be based on nothing more startling than the fact that there is more than one of us on the planet and we have to work out ways of managing that. We have a mutual obligation. Our lives are guided by reciprocity. To live together with respect for, and ease with, each other we owe each other a duty of care. In the eighteenth century even a selfish bugger like the philosopher David Hume recognised that this was a duty that arose beyond generosity. In *A Treatise of Human Nature* of 1740 he wrote, 'I learn to do service to another, without bearing him any real kindness: because I foresee, that he will return my service, in expectation of another of the same kind . . .' Manners are not necessarily an exercise in altruism.They are a form of self-interest because they breed reciprocity. Whether driven by selfishness or selflessness manners are a question of ethics. Behaviour which takes not just our own desires into account, but balances them against other people's, requires us to impose on ourselves some restraint for the greater good. It implies the presence in our lives of an 'ought' and an 'ought not'. It says that there is certain behaviour that is, and certain that isn't, the done thing.

My parents' generation used that phrase. The done thing. It was the done thing to curtsey in specific ways. Yes, to pass the port to the left. To wear your wedding ring on a particular finger. To seat people at your dinner table in a designated order, to use a butter knife, not to hold your ordinary knife in this way but in that way, and not to do *this* and certainly to do *that*. So it went on. And the sanction was class. You were looked down upon if you didn't know what was the done thing. This was dizzying in its snobbery and rococo in the intensity of its detail. Life, particularly social life, was a maze designed by the middle and upper classes in which new money and the working class were condemned to wander without help, endlessly mocked, if not always out loud, by those who knew the secrets of the puzzle.

The trouble for manners is that they have been vastly discredited by the etiquette brigade. They have set up a series of tripwires, mainly for the working class, but also for the rest of us who simply had neither the time nor the desire to find out the exact weight and size of an invitation card which *Debrett's New Guide to Etiquette and Modern Manners – The Indispensable Handbook*, however, has. I know you'll be hunched in gratitude if I tell you – and write it down, mind – that, according to *Debrett's*, it's six hundred grammes and five and a half inches by seven. But be honest; who really cares if some posh tot has decided that 'bananas must never be eaten monkey-style at the table'? Or that you know 'how to entertain royalty'? And yes, one entire section of *Debrett's* is devoted to precisely that. Should you have sleepless nights worrying about how to address the wife of a viscount's son, you will again be abject to discover it is different on an envelope from the beginning of the letter and from when talking to them in person or – and once more I can hear your sighs of gratitude as you're saved from committing yet another socially humiliating *faux pas* – the place card. And if you didn't already know that, just how have you managed to struggle through your life this far? More than fifty years ago Amy Vanderbilt, in her *Complete Book of Etiquette*, managed to write an entire explanation of how a man ought to behave with his hat. It's rather beautiful, in fact very elegant. She says:

> In greeting a woman friend in the street or in some public place, once she has bowed first, a man actually lifts his hat from his head, turning his head slightly toward the woman and smiling, if he wishes, but not stopping unless she stops first. He must certainly not stop dead in his tracks and stare after her. If they do stop and talk, he should guide his companion out of the way of traffic after shaking hands — if she has made the first gesture to do so. He may return his hat to his head without apology if they are in the open and weather is bad, but he must not smoke.

And when men wore a lot of headgear I imagine all that was a life-saver, especially if you were about to marry a woman whose love for you was only so strong that she would leave you at the drop of a hat. It's not that these rules weren't comforting to the people who knew them. They were. But to the people who didn't know them they were another reason to be looked down on.

But the done things in our behaviour with one another should be based not on rules driven by class or gender drawn from a particular age, but rather on ones drawn from principle which we can see from our anthropology and history have underpinned our social relationships with each other. And there are actually not too many of them that matter. The ones that do sit like friendly pink elephants in the middle of the room, so obvious are they. When we think about it we're hard pushed not to see them.

How we eat together is based on the simple premise that it's not about the food, it's about the company. Despite our current love affair with the charms of the culinary, the food is the least important element of sitting round a table together. Rather, we are. People commune over food. We express our friendship, we settle disputes and we celebrate.

At weddings and commitment ceremonies the froth and bother expended on the desperate desire for white wedding correctness obscure the elevating and inspiring notion that the only two things that really matter are the vows and the fact that they are witnessed. These are what bind us to one another in love and to our friends and families in asking them to stand guarantors for our happiness. How far back in the church your cousin sits and whether you have a present list or not fades just a touch in comparison. At funerals the question of what clothes you wear falls back to a very distant second place behind honouring the dead and comforting the bereaved.

When we talk to each other it is a journey of exploration that is only human. Never mind how superficial and momentary, even you and the bus driver can have a second of humanity over the change. And when you encounter people you do not know and you want to, then manners simply suggests some ways of making it easier to do so through conversation.

Work defines us. Yet many of its guiding narratives are being destabilised by the demands of constant change. This creates enormous vulnerability for us. Old certainties at work have faded. We are in competition with our fellow workers yet also exhorted to bond in teams with them. The formality of manners and an absence of management consultancy bullshit might make navigating through work slightly more certain in an uncertain world. Manners at work demand clarity from our bosses, not mateyness.

And in love? Well, in love there are rules. You'll find only three here in this book. Don't ever hurt them physically or emotionally. Always be faithful to them. And never leave the loo seat up. But when you're in love or you've fallen out of love or they have, you're so potty, so mad, so deranged, so completely out of control, there really is very little chance of you sticking to them.

From history, anthropology and culture we can deduce some principles and we can apply them. And we can have fun doing it. But if we are able to decide on some rules our most difficult task comes after that. There is a huge question about how we enforce that agreement with each other. Now that we have, to the great relief of many of us, dispensed with any agreement that our guiding light is either Our Maker, Our Monarch or just Men, we are left to do the job ourselves. Now that we have inherited the immoral consequences of getting on our bikes to find work, geographical communities are far more fluid. There has been an unprecedented level of change in the roles and expectations of women. Sexuality has burst from the underground and our society is vastly less culturally monochrome than it has been. So it is now more difficult to forge a consensus around particular behaviour and more of a problem to enforce it. None of which, though, can obscure the simple fact that 'please' and 'thank you' in the array of their varying expression cross all bounds of race, sexuality, gender and class. Please is universally polite, however it's expressed. And thank you is a gift in any language.

We have a crisis of authority. We deplore the behaviour of so many people on the streets. And not just the young. We are overrun by the selfishness of the middle-class driver who ploughs into the yellow crisscrosses regardless of the log jam he creates. We are beset by suburban families who dump their trash on the pavement outside their own garden fence for someone else to clear away. We are bruised by the verbal violence of chav-nots rampaging through our lives. We are angered by the friends who stay in our houses without making any contribution. We are ground down by thoughtlessness rollerblading over our sensitivities, shouting on its mobile and having no care for the rest of us.

Yet we feel powerless to do anything about it. From the Royal family to footballers our role models have shirked the responsibility we give them in exchange for their position. Prince Charles has lost the last shreds of moral authority as he lives a romantic life which prevents him from marrying in a church of which he will one day be the head. Footballers swear their way to million pound bank balances, their defiance of the referee keeping the money flowing and the fans in tow. We are left scared to challenge bad manners in private or public for fear of being thought old fashioned or illiberal.

Manners have fallen into disrepute because in the face of all this they have a problem of credibility. What too many people mean by manners has become encrusted by the barnacles, baubles and gothic detail of etiquette, forged by Gods, Kings and Boys. We need to return them to their basic and human function. We need to sound a rallying call for true civility. If you're up for it then this has to be the start of a campaign. We have to initiate a rampage of civil obedience. And be prepared to back it up. We have to be our own guarantors of good manners to each other. Etiquette always reminds me of the worst kinds of bureaucracy. It is mountains of petty details piled high to give uninteresting people as many reasons as they can find to deny other people the possibility of achieving their goals. It is the squeaky nasal voice of the professional gainsayer. Manners, however, are a constitution, the fundamental principles of how we might live together. Our job is to reinterpret and apply them for our own age. In a different context, Hartley Shawcross said in 1946 after the Labour victory, 'we are the masters at the moment'. And in the twenty-first century, we must now be the masters for manners.

At the start of our new century we are at a point with manners that has been reached before. On the first occasion, in the early sixteenth century, there emerged a more powerful and cultured bourgeoisie in Europe who raised an intellectual challenge to the Courts' claim to be the sole arbiters of fashion and behaviour. And then again on the cusp of the eighteenth century in Britain after the Revolution, as the Court moved out of London, the upheaval in the traditional seat of power left the field of the discussion of behaviour open to intellectuals rather than courtiers. In both cases social change thrust manners to the centre of the debate about a person's quality as a human being and they became the way that you found your place not at Court but in the world.

When Erasmus wrote his pamphlet 'On Good Manners For Boys' in 1530, he was doing something quite extraordinary. It is short, no more than a few thousand words. But its impact was immense. It was reprinted thirty times in his lifetime and in all there have been one hundred and thirty editions, the last one as recent as the eighteenth century. It was first translated into English two years after it appeared in its original Latin. The seven chapters in Erasmus's book, which have guided the divisions of the one you are reading, cover the body; dress; behaviour in church; behaviour at banquets; meeting people; play; and the bedroom. The significance, though, is not just that it was so obviously popular, but that someone of such remarkable intellect thought that to write about manners was not at all beneath him. Norbert Elias, who published the groundbreaking *History of Manners* as part of a project on 'the civilising process' in the late 1930s, argues that an intellectual as renowned as Erasmus writing about the subject of conduct is a sign of the times and demonstrates that 'the problem of behaviour in society had obviously taken on such importance in this period that even people of extraordinary talent and renown did not disdain to concern themselves with it'. More than that, while Erasmus sees that 'the real nurseries of what is regarded as good manners in his time are the princely courts', he also has sufficient standing and independence to criticise the rules when they are just courtly and serve no greater purpose. And he explicitly writes his treatise, which was addressed to Henry Burgundy, the eleven-year-old son of Adolph Prince of Vere, as a declaration of much broader values of civility, to be followed and aspired to by all people. While he writes about how to stand, and eat and talk, how to blow your nose and use your knife, he is quite explicit that the standard of this behaviour speaks to the whole man: 'Although this outward bodily propriety proceeds from a well-composed mind, nevertheless we sometimes find that, for want of instruction, such grace is lacking in excellent and learned men.' In other words you can be born as posh as you like and still be ill-mannered, and whatever the circumstances of your birth manners can be learned.

Early on in his first chapter Erasmus makes a brave statement for the time which distances himself from the ruling elite: 'Let others paint lions, eagles, bulls and leopards on their coats of arms. More true nobility is possessed by those who can inscribe on their shields all that they have achieved through the cultivation of the arts and sciences.' It is a moving declaration of the profound value of good behaviour and manners to the quality of a person. And all the more so perhaps because, six years before his death, and in poor health, this great scholar was turning his mind to the start of the adult life of a young man to whom he had chosen to give the benefit of his wisdom and what he observed about how to go well in the world.

We sometimes struggle rather with the concept of manners, because it's often taken to mean the difference between so-called civilised behaviour and uncivilised behaviour. And these two tend to be deployed as if they were opposites. Like good and evil, black and white, good taste and Liberace. So, while we feel the burn of the censorious judgement of those who tell us we have bad manners, they seem to be doing it more to prove that they know something that we don't. To set themselves above. To make themselves out to be 'more civilised' than us. Certainly that tone of voice is unmistakeable in the talk of etiquette around the smart tables of Britain even today. But these people are not doing as Erasmus was: adding to the wellbeing of the society in which he lived. They are merely trying to show that they are somehow better. But to call someone's behaviour 'civilised' or 'uncivilised' is not truly to make a judgement about quality. They are not opposite poles. They are, rather, points on a journey, 'stages of development' as Elias calls them, which, as he demonstrated, is part of a process that is still continuing. This is not some sloppy-haired plea for relativism. You know, the kind of thing where people suggest that there is no right and wrong, just a series of different rights. There is right and wrong, but that's not what we're concerned about with the idea of civilisation. Civilised and uncivilised are not synonyms for right and wrong when it comes to behaviour.

We look back at what we were and call it uncivilised without the perspective of our distant future successors who will find things that we do now uncivilised. What you see in the Middle Ages, and certainly around Erasmus's time, for instance, is an almost complete lack of embarrassment about bodily functions. Whereas we are quite squeamish about them. A whole section of one episode of *Sex and the City* was devoted to whether a new man could be dumped for dumping without discretion. They couldn't help but wonder, as Carrie Bradshaw might have put it: should one close the door on a relationship if they don't close the door on a poo? Since the sixteenth century bodily functions – and if I add to the word poo, 'weeing' and 'bonking', the euphemisms will make the point – have been largely removed from 'polite' conversation.

There's a wonderful example of this contrast in a pamphlet written in 1568. In Mathew Cordier's *Dialogues for Schoolboys* a young chap is asked to say what he did between getting up and having breakfast. He tells his teacher: 'I woke up, got out of bed, put on my shirt, stockings and shoes, buckled my belt, urinated against the courtyard wall . . .' – Sorry? You did what? – '. . . urinated against the courtyard wall, took fresh water from the bucket, washed my hands and face . . .' and so on. This child reports his widdle in exactly the same beat as buckling his belt and putting on his shirt. If a child at school did that today, he'd be accused of being cheeky. In fact, of taking the piss. But not then.

It may well be the case that in as many years to come, in 2442, our descendants will look at our smoking or perhaps the openness with which we discuss sex and personal relationships on TV, as very curiously 'uncivilised' behaviour, which breaks all sorts of taboos which by then will have built up through the changed social circumstances of the preceding four hundred-odd years. They will read with complete incredulity that we lit tobacco and, in spaces shared with other people, blew it in their faces. And even that in one phase of our civilised twentieth century it was thought to be a sign of deep sexual attraction. These taboos grow up around changes in technology, like sewers, or new understandings about health such as the prohibition on spitting which flowed from the discovery of the TB bacillus. The notion of civilised behaviour doesn't only use taboos. It also has, for instance, produced, in not too distant times, an idea that delicacy or refinement is more civilised. The more, for example, the rich could hold their knives and forks with the lightest of grips, the more they showed that they had other people, their servants, to prepare their food for them. From this, ridiculous, display of 'delicacy' flows the now laugh-able sign of social superiority when a person holds their tea cup with their pinkie sticking out. This is snobbery not civilisation. It's shocking to us but intellectually sobering to remember that Renaissance Italy painted, sculpted and created divinely at what we consider one of the peaks of civilisation, but also pissed openly in the street and even in the corners of rooms. To a great extent we are prey to the arrogance of the nineteenth century and the Victorians. As the Court gave way to the city, courtesy to civility, eventually a notion took root in the nineteenth century, not just in Britain although strongly here, that the process of civilisation had been completed and the only people who really needed it were foreigners and the working class. Which was the most tragic betrayal of the ideas of politeness which in the eighteenth century had made London the very centre of a revolution in manners.

When Dr Johnson said, 'When a man is tired of London he is tired of life; for there is in London all that life can afford', he wasn't prefiguring a London with *Les Mis*, *Mamma Mia!*, the Groucho Club and Gordon Ramsay restaurants. He was talking about a city that had a genuine hold not just over the country but, as the historian John Brewer put it, over the English imagination. Not only did 10 per cent of the country live there, one in six of the population worked there, it was ten times larger than any other city in Britain and, again, as Brewer writes in *The Pleasures of the Imagination*, 'Nowhere else in Britain was so urban; no other city quite so exciting and shocking.' And in large part this was because 'polite' society had moved beyond the control and creation of the Court. Charles I had been a great patron, a cultured supporter and commissioner of art and writing. His Court might bicker and fight but they were essentially a cultured lot, ceding their petty political battles to an organising cultural force. But then he got his head chopped off. (Might as well cut to the chase.) And Cromwell wasn't as much a lover of the arts as he might have been. Save Milton and Marvell, the Puritan regime didn't stimulate that much of a cultural contribution. But what they had done was weaken the Court and democratise the country. In 1698 the Palace at Whitehall went up in flames and the Court moved out of the centre of London to Kensington. There was no real stage for the Crown to play culture on. Driven by the increasing prosperity of the time, London became that stage and people other than courtiers started to strut on it.

The country was divided by religion and political party. After the Revolution the monarchy was constitutionally bound to Parliament and it was a political world that we might just recognise. There emerged in London little crucibles of debate, places of conviviality which became the lubricators of social intercourse. London's coffee houses were the places in which people gossiped and and drank and argued and plotted. They were, crucially, not restricted like the Court. When you sat down you had no immediate idea of the provenance of the person you spoke to. Were they a Whig, a Tory, a Protestant or a Catholic? Were they noble or clever, rich or poor or all of those things or none? Actually, if they weren't at least bright and a bit sharp you get the impression that they probably had to sit in the corner and do macramé or a puzzle book or some eighteenth-century equivalent.

The best for them was to hang on everybody else's conversation. But generally the coffee houses displayed what Brewer calls 'a disconcertingly egalitarian ethos'. And the novelist Samuel Butler sniffily remarked, 'the coffee house proprietor admits of no distinction of persons'. The throne had been usurped not so much by Parliament as by conversation. The classes who chattered became the generators of controversy, fashion and taste. So, of course, in 1675 Charles II tried to close all the coffee houses down. Fat chance. He failed. By the time of Queen Anne's reign in the early eighteenth century Joseph Addison, who with Richard Steele started the *Spectator* and the *Tatler*, was able to write in the ninth number of the *Spectator*, 'When men are thus knit together, by a Love of Society, and not by a Spirit of Faction, and don't meet to censure or annoy those that are absent, but to enjoy one another; When they are thus combined for their own Improvement, or for the Good of others, or at least to relax themselves from the Business of the Day, by an innocent and chearful Conversation, there may be something very useful in these little Institutions and Establishments.'

The coffee houses in turn bred clubs and societies. And what emerged from Dr Johnson's Literary Club and, probably the most influential one, the Kit-Cat Club, which was named after Christopher Cat, the landlord of the Cat and Fiddle in Gray's Inn Lane, was a notion of culture closely related to an idea of politeness. The importance of that for any discussion of manners is that in the context of a society riven by division what was emerging was a desire for harmony between people who disagreed. This is a whole new idea. We, sometimes happily and sometimes in absolute frustration, are nonetheless used to ending an argument by 'agreeing to disagree'. In the eighteenth century this was a concept as new to them as the ability to talk across the globe instantaneously through the cyber connection of the internet is still to us. It changed their discourse. Fundamentally, in the eighteenth century it produced an idea of 'politeness' which guided behaviour between strangers.

Manners ebb and flow between the strictness and fussy detail of courts and ruling elites and the desire of us the common people – and please don't take offence at being called common; I merely mean that you're not royalty or a courtier – to talk and live and work together in ways that treat ourselves and our opinions with respect. Manners are always subject to an authority. The question is whether that authority is an elite or whether manners are determined by a debate across society. Erasmus wrote in a time of social change, where power ebbed from the Court towards intellect and debate. Similarly, in eighteenth-century England, the monarch had receded as the focus of taste and opinion. The *Spectator* and its readers disseminated an idea of politeness which, as Addison had indicated in his praise of the coffee houses, was about a love of society. To quote Brewer once more, 'The aim of politeness was to reach an accommodation with the complexities of modern life and to replace political zeal and religious bigotry with mutual tolerance and understanding. The means of achieving this was a manner of conversing and dealing with people which, by teaching one to regulate one's passions and to cultivate good taste, would enable a person to realise what was in the public interest and for the general good.'

So how the hell did that get twisted into the right way to eat a banana at table and the weight of a wedding invitation?

Well, what happens too often is that manners get perverted from a framework of sociability into a set of weapons for social exclusion. We shouldn't kid ourselves that Addison and Steele's notion of politeness was democratic. We are still talking about a relatively limited stratum of society, but at least entry to it was down to little more than whether you could afford the price of admission to Vauxhall Gardens for a promenade. Politeness was to a great degree a public occupation. The pleasure gardens in the mid-eighteenth century were transformed from places that were risky to ones that were respectable. But, of course, as soon as everyone is able to be polite – and from Erasmus to Addison it is always the point that manners and good conduct are open to instruction – the elite moves in and starts to reclaim the territory. Rules are invented to make sure that strangers are spotted. And the figures of fun emerge. Snobbery, a great English game, rises from the embers of the incinerated Court and, for instance in the eighteenth century, the gentleman farmers and the provincials became the butt of the jokes of society. In the battle for power in which the elite fight to the last defining detail to retain the upper hand new distinctions are introduced to the disadvantage of those below. As fast as people of humbler origins climb up the social ladder through wealth and prosperity, those at the top climb even faster. For every single rung the gentleman farmer mounted, the viscount mounted two. If you can buy your way into the gentry, they will in turn find ways of saying that you don't really belong there. And the way they do that is to start inventing rules about bananas and invitations.

You know the old line – and perm any northern or provincial town into it at your convenience: 'You can take the girl out of Macclesfield but you can't take Macclesfield out of the girl.' Well, it's a pretty explicit expression of that notion of breeding. As soon as manners become open to instruction, the ruling elite has to fall back on an idea that, while someone can learn to hold their knife and fork 'properly', they will still be discoverd to be lacking, to be ersatz class-wise, even if they have the money to take them into the upper echelons. They will be spotted as a result of something inherent in the provenance of their birth. This, of course, despite the fact that only a few generations back most aristocrats were themselves mere soldiers rewarded by the monarch.

But manners do not flow from class. Lots of customs do. The middle classes say sofa, napkin, drawing room, hold their teacup with pinkie in, do not use doilies and never say cruet. The working class say settee, serviette, front room or lounge, often hold their cup pinkie out when the vicar calls and boast about their cruets. None of which has anything to do with manners. Manners are a way of behaving. They sometimes recognise taboos, as in the case of eating with your mouth closed, but more often than not they are about that simple recognition that consideration shown to others is the best behaviour, that food is to be shared, that space is to be negotiated, that selfish desires are to be restrained in the general good. And they flow from instruction.

It is one of the most obvious and poignant elements

of Erasmus's text that he has such confidence in the ability of the young man to whom he is writing to see the social sense of what he is saying. For manners to be enforced we have to feel a certain amount of shame about their breach. We have to know that there is a social sanction. And that has to start with parents teaching it to their children. That is where we first learn the idea of restraint. Children don't need to be taught the rules according to *Debrett's*. They are just the clues to a treasure hunt in which the prize is merely social acceptability into a certain class. Children need to grow up sensing that if they are unconscious of others, entirely selfish and without consideration, they lack manners. And that there is a sense of disapproval if they behave like that. They do not need to learn the intricate details of etiquette. This was surely what Erasmus had in mind when he wrote, 'No one can choose his own parents or nationality, but each can mould his own talents and character for himself . . . the essence of good manners consists in freely pardoning the shortcomings of others although nowhere falling short yourself: in holding a companion no less dear because his standards are less exacting.'

—⚏—

FORMAL OCCASIONS

WEDDINGS

In following Erasmus I have interpreted his chapter headings rather freely to suit my own purpose. Forgive me. But he was such a wise old bird; what he writes retains enormous resonance. You don't have to stray too far for it to ring immediate bells for us. He begins his second chapter, on dress, by saying the following: 'Clothing is in a way the body's body, and from this too one may infer the state of a man's character. And yet no fixed rule can be laid down on this matter, because everyone does not have the same fortune or rank and standards of what is becoming and what is not differ among nations.' It is a gentle and wise rebuke to those who insist that there is only one way to dress, and thus to behave, at those moments that have in the past become dangerously formalised – our rites of passage. When someone came up with the phrase 'hatches, matches and dispatches' to try and give a bit of idiomatic glamour to the otherwise entirely tedious business of slogging away at your first job as a journalist, they got the list in one. The only rite of passage they missed was that rather tricky moment of transition from childhood to adulthood which, in our patriarchal world, is mainly celebrated for boys. They get confirmed, if they're Christian, Bar Mitzvahed, if they're Jewish and circumcised, if they're unlucky. Because at that age it just hurts.

The two that retain the greatest importance are, of course, weddings and funerals. Erasmus guides us towards making our own rules. And I'll concentrate on them. Baptisms, even naming ceremonies, are so uncommon that I certainly can't remember when I last went to one. There is little that is formal now about birth or god-parenting. Mainly because, despite the inclusion of the word God in the title even by the irreligious, few people put the birth of their child down to divine intervention, or even supervision, any more. Religion has largely lost its pull on reproduction, at least in Britain. Although there are women who think that, after the amount of alcohol their partner consumed on the night of conception, the pregnancy might legitimately be regarded as a miracle.

Richard Curtis was no fool. Weddings and funerals are what we care about. And the movie's title gives roughly the right proportions to the anxiety most people expend on each. It's about 4:1. Almost always at short notice, we feel that funerals just have to be organised and got through. They are regarded as ghastly, inevitable, better not talked about and best when brief. They seem to happen less frequently than weddings, although statistically that's simply not possible. It's probably because we try and avoid them. But, as we'll see later, they can in fact be an impeccable combination of ritual and individuality that brings out the very best in each of us and shows us manners at their most telling.

Weddings, on the other hand, are regarded as wonderful, certainly not inevitable, to be talked about endlessly, both before and after, and best when they go on for months, compulsorily seeming to involve showers, stag dos, rehearsal dinners, receptions, dances and, the next day, even a wedding breakfast. The celebrating can last longer than the relationship itself.

Some people just don't seem to take them seriously. The wedding with the least staying power on record at the moment is the showbiz marriage of Britney Spears, whom your children will know is an internationally famous pop sensation, to someone called Jason Allen Alexander, who was a school friend and seems mainly to be known just to his mum and dad. They got married in Las Vegas on a Saturday in January 2004 and started annulment proceedings after fifty-five hours on the following Monday morning. It still vies in the history of entertainment with Rudolph Valentino's marriage to Jean Acker in 1919. After six hours, according to Hollywood legend, she apparently locked him out of the honeymoon suite. And he just gave up and went home. But they didn't actually get a divorce for twenty-two months. Cher married Greg Allman three days after divorcing Sonny Bono but then left him nine days later. And Elizabeth Taylor has said 'till death do us part' so many times now, it makes you believe in the afterlife.

But even when taken seriously marriage is still on the decline in Britain according to the Office of National Statistics. There were 45 per cent fewer first-time marriages in 2000 than there were in 1950. It rallied a bit in 1970 as a result of the post-war baby boom and hit a peak of 390,000 but that had then dropped to 179,000 by 1999. Divorce experienced an equal but opposite trajectory. However, despite this statistical blizzard of bad news for the traditionalists, the last census still tells us that 50 per cent of men and women are married and only 10 per cent are cohabiting. And weddings are still regarded, of course, not just as romantically important but, according to the UK Alliance of Wedding Planners (can you believe that?), weddings.co.uk and the *Guardian*, they are worth spending £12,000 on. Which is half the average UK annual salary.

Ever since Herodotus, the Greek storyteller and some say the first historian and anthropologist, told of the promiscuity of various peoples across the world – the Libyans, the Samoans and the lotus-eating Lotophagi of North Africa subsequently immortalised by Tennyson – there have been arguments about whether promiscuity or marriage was the natural state of human existence. By the late nineteenth century the Finnish anthropologist Edvard Westermarck, who's of help here because he wrote the standard work, his doctoral thesis *The History of Human Marriage*, in 1891, spent some time and hundreds of pages arguing against the notion that it was. It had become the accepted wisdom of anthropological study by those writing at the time, men such as Bachofen, Lubbock and Giraud-Teulon, that the original sexual relationship among practically all peoples was different forms of promiscuity, polyandry and polygamy. That theory was, according to Westermarck, treated by many writers as a demonstrated truth. All those savage people, they thought, merrily taking as many wives or husbands as they wanted, which conclusion proved presumably to the stern nineteenth century that it was far more civilised than these primitives. Starting from Darwin's premiss, however, Westermarck set out to prove that monogamy – marriage and stable couples – was the fundamental building block of social organisation. And it's perhaps of only incidental curiosity that his arguments were also true to his own life, as he lived for many years in England with the philosopher and psychologist James Sully.

This short deviation is absolutely not to enter the argument about whether marriage is the only form of stable relationship. Clearly it isn't. But when trying to consider what manners might guide us through the celebration of marriage it's worth having a stab at asking, what about marriage is fundamental and what is decoration? The traditions, which many of us have come to think of as the key elements of a standard British wedding, have often simply grown out of and been adapted over the years from pagan customs. The carrying of a wedding bouquet, for instance, originated in Roman times with the bride, who must have consequently ended up looking slightly like a salad, wearing flowers and herbs all over her dress in order to ward off evil spirits. Similarly, men at weddings have dressed the same, sometimes in military uniform, sometimes in the clothes of their trade (certainly since the Middle Ages) because it was the superstition that you needed to frighten evil spirits away from the couple getting married. And the best way to do that was thought to be to confuse these clearly rather soft-headed demons by dressing the bridesmaids and the groomsmen like the bride and groom themselves so the nasties couldn't tell the happy couple from everybody else. This habit in some weddings then spread to the guests. These days the bride's excitement has got the better of her and she wears an even nicer frock than her girlfriends. But what you actually wear in order to fulfil this convention then varies according to fashion, whether it's the formal tuxedo in America or the morning dress beloved of the British middle class, which is essentially just the smartest thing available to wear, because it was the nineteenth- and early twentieth-century ceremonial dress at Court.

At the centre of weddings has always been their function as a building block of social organisation. When *The Economist* ran a front page in January 1996 with the headline 'Let Them Wed', at the time considered controversial, in favour of gay marriage, it did so not because it had suddenly developed a new enthusiasm for human rights and equality but because the magazine argued that it was fundamental to the stability of society to allow people to form lasting bonds with each other and have them recognised. It spoke more to property and stability than it did to ideology. It was an intriguing argument, though, because it reached over the head of the angry screeches of the controversy in the Church by seeking to strengthen one of the fundamental units of society by simply extending its scope to all. The controversy rages on. But it does illustrate not least the extent to which, while religion claims marriage as its own, others claim it as something more secular. In 1539, in the Reformation, Luther, mainly for pragmatic reasons of anti-papist politics and the defence of the Protestant Church against Rome, even gave his blessing and justification to the bigamous marriage of the splendidly named Philip the Magnanimous, declaring that marriage was not a sacrament but a worldly thing. This was a profound challenge to the original Christian notion of marriage as sacred and not just a contract, which was what St Paul asserted when he compared the relationship of a husband and wife to that of Christ and his Church in the Epistle to the Ephesians (v, 23–32).

St Paul vs Luther is just one of many attempts to own marriage and weddings, some of them very recent. And many have tried to restrict who may marry. One of the most disgraceful was the banning of interracial marriage in America, only finally wiped off the statute books of all the states by the Supreme Court in 1967. This led, the next time the Supreme Court considered the issue of who could marry – in that case incarcerated prisoners – to its listing in its judgement four key attributes of marriage: the expression of emotional support and public commitment; a spiritual significance, and for some the exercise of a religious faith; the expectation that, for most, the marriage would be consummated; and the receipt of tangible benefits, including government benefits and property rights.

The romance of walking down the aisle is beginning to feel a little strained in the light of that legalese. What concerns most of us is not the function of marriage but the joys of the wedding ceremony, the dress, the place, the reception, the sheer excitement of it all. But if we are to try and chart a steady course through weddings and devise some modern manners for the ceremony we will first need to try and identify for ourselves the central elements. Because there is an awful lot of energy expended on a huge range of questions which may in the end be guided not by manners or principle but rather by simple personal choice. It may be that where you choose to marry, what you choose to wear or whether you put a silver sixpence in your shoe is in the end really down to you.

Nonetheless, we take the details of weddings very seriously and we plan them like the 8th Army assault on Rommel. The wealthy employ teams of organisers to advance them towards their nuptial El Alamein, presumably drawn from the formidable sounding UK Alliance of Wedding Planners. And even the poorest of us spend days worrying about the frocks and the corsages. In the seventeenth edition of her standard work *Etiquette*, Emily Post dedicates 184 pages to weddings, there are more than two thousand books on Amazon on how to organise your perfect wedding, and about sixty-three million entries for 'wedding' on Google. Someone somewhere thinks that *how* you do it is terribly important.

Brides and mainly their mothers worry hugely about whether they're getting it right. And, of course, it's they who do the fretting. (Fathers still seem to play golf or go to the pub during most of it.) And their anxiety reaches new levels of detail. Agony aunts are deluged with questions, Miss Manners' syndicated column in American newspapers overwhelmed with letters, subscriptions are taken out to the hundreds of wedding magazines on sale in newsagents. Mothers and daughters want to know what food to serve, what to wear, what not to wear, whom to ask, whom not to ask, whether to mention wedding presents or not.

Should we include the present list with the invitations? Does that seem greedy? Should we announce the engagement and, if so, how? They agitate about the significance of the cake, the flowers, the ring, the attendants, the colours of the dresses, who gives the bride away, who arrives last at the church, who pays for what, whether you can wear white if you're not a virgin. Whether guests will snigger if you do. Whether your three-year-old can be the bridesmaid. Can your dog be the witness? (Honestly.) And so on. And the etiquette books and magazines and internet sites work overtime to answer the questions. But when you set the traditional Church of England wedding alongside many of the ceremonies from other cultures and religions you begin to see how the central elements of a wedding have some consistency, while the particular practices differ according to culture and faith.

The centuries-old Ukrainian wedding ceremony seems to involve a lot of bread, according to Natalie Kononenko, Professor of Slavic Languages, Literatures, and Folklore at the University of Virginia. On the engagement, the groom's family visits the bride's and takes a loaf. (Incidentally, if you ever get a proposal from a Ukrainian and you want to reject it, you are apparently advised to take a pumpkin to give in exchange for this bread. Although it does seem a bit harsh to wait until the groom arrives on your doorstep. And then to say it with vegetables and not even flowers.) Then, on the Thursday or Friday before the actual wedding, a special bread called a *korovai* is baked. And then on Saturday morning the bride and groom walk through the village with yet another ritual bread called the *shyshka*. In fact, unless you are gluten-intolerant, Ukrainian weddings sound a lot of fun. The formal part is followed by a period of 'mischief' which can involve running through the village stealing chickens and other food, the leading tractor driver in the village dressing in drag, and even pulling a cart with the bride's parents in it to the nearest river and dumping them in the water. The whole ritual puts a great deal of emphasis on cementing the union between the bride and the groom in order to perpetuate their families and the village.

WeblinkIndia's huge wedding directory, Matrimonials India, describes eleven different religious wedding rituals. Hindu weddings are held around a fire constantly fed with ghee. The bride and groom are tied together with a knot made of her dress and his *chadar* and they then take the *saat pheras*, the seven vows, by going around the fire seven times. With their hands clasped together these seven steps symbolise their journey through life together: the first step for a long married life; the second for power; the third for prosperity; the fourth for happiness; the fifth for welfare of children; the sixth for enjoyment or pleasure; and the seventh for lifelong friendship. Much of the focus is on 'tying the knot', a long-standing symbol of weddings, clearly visible in the Renaissance ceremony of 'handfasting' in which couples pledge their betrothal by joining hands, his right to her right, his left to her left, so from above they looked like an infinity symbol.

Muslim weddings can last five days and involve the exchange of many gifts. Traditions tend to be influenced by the region in which the wedding takes place. In south India, the bride gets a necklace called a *lachha* from the groom, for instance, but in the north she gets a nose ring. But the basics are pretty much the same. Dowries and alimonies are exchanged, the girl is anointed with turmeric, the couple dine with the parents of the bride on the fifth day and in the spirit of fairness it is an Islamic custom that the bride's parents shouldn't suffer financially. So the costs are shared between the families.

In Parsi weddings there is more of the number seven. The couple sit opposite each other and a cloth is wound around their chairs to create a circle. The ends of the cloth are then tied together in a knot. The priest places the right hands of the bride and groom together and fastens them with a raw twist seven times. The twist is then passed around the couple seven times and then seven times around the knot in the cloth, as prayers are recited.

None of this ever happens in even the smartest churches in Hampshire. Instead, mainly in June and July, country churches throughout the Home Counties and the South of England are crammed with people who more often see the inside of the London Stock Exchange or an army barracks in far-flung climes than the vestry of Little Sloshingham-on-the-Marsh. And they are dressed beyond the nines to at least the tens or elevens in an anachronistic impression of a set of Edwardian bankers. In morning dress they parade like penguins basking in self-satisfaction. And when there's any kind of Scottish connection the sartorial display of Hooray tartan is a dazzling mix of greens, reds, blues and yellows, enough to make a chameleon wear sunglasses. Some of them look like they have fallen into a dressing up box for a bet. The women wear dresses that look like food and hats the size of the rings round Saturn. Some of them seem to have Peter Scott's entire Slimbridge bird sanctuary on their heads.

My point is not to mock – and, hands up, I admit that I too have fallen into that posh dressing-up box more than once – but to illustrate that, while we all want definitive guidance about what to do at a wedding, there is not so much to base it on. In fact, the traditions that have grown up around different weddings in different cultures all clothe two fundamental elements of a wedding in bright, glorious, exuberant details of frocks and rings and cakes and churches and hats and flowers, all of which are open to us to choose. The two key elements of weddings are the contract you make with each other and the witnessing of it by family and friends. At the centre of the ceremony is the relationship between two people and how the rest of us honour that. Weddings – and at this point we should include commitment ceremonies – and funerals allow us rituals that confirm our interdependence with each other. Vows sincerely meant and made in front of others are a confirmation that we live in a world where there is more than one of us. At weddings and commitments we are both participants in, and observers and guarantors of, each other's happiness. When they feel right they can reassure the rest of us of our own potential for love. They temporarily banish cynicism and pessimism in favour of sincere hope, although that may not have been true of the wedding of two of his Oxford graduates at which Maurice Bowra was apocryphally said to have remarked: 'It'll never work. I've slept with both of them and, I tell you, it'll never work.'

The wedding ceremony in its essence intertwines

the couple with their families and, increasingly these days, with their friends. While our contemporary romantic logic might suggest that it should be about the bride and groom, in fact we all know that symbolically, and often in reality, it isn't. Brides have been heard to complain that they want the kind of wedding *they* want. And mothers have been known to answer that they'll get that when they have a daughter of their own. But more than that, while weddings may have a romantic core of two people falling in love, in a culture or religion where marriages are arranged that is not necessarily the whole truth. Anthropologically weddings have never been wholly about the individuals: they've been about the alliances between kinship groups. Less academically put, that means families for most of us and, for those of you reading this who are rulers and monarchs, a few centuries ago it probably meant your country. The list of kings, queens and aristocrats who married for power, money and to secure the succession is endless. Henry VIII was no oddball in having a fondness for strategic wives or ones who might produce not just an heir but also the right kind – a son. And almost five hundred years later there was much gossip about Prince Charles's search for a suitable bride for his 'fairytale wedding'. Princess Diana was sighted, stalked, trapped and bagged by a royal family as keen on hunting for suitable spouses as they are not terribly good at it. Billed as a great romantic match, we now know that in fact the marriage was a rather crowded misalliance from the very beginning. It nonetheless, of course, produced the required strapping heirs.

But you don't have to be royal to have your marriage options circumscribed and romance confined to a more limited field. The Aborigines, for instance, have a strict set of codes about whom you should and shouldn't marry. You are born into a 'marriage group'. The Aboriginal Education Department of South Australia identifies the eight of them as Panunga, Purula, Appungerta, Kumara, Uknaria, Ungalla, Bulthara and Umbitchana. A man from the Panunga has to marry a woman from the Purula group and their kids, boys and girls, will belong to the Appungerta. And vice versa. Male Purulas must marry a female Panunga. Except their children will be Kumara. An Appungerta must marry an Umbitchana. And so on. But although the spelling of the names may take a short while to master, if you're reading this anywhere north of Ayers Rock, or more properly Uluru, it's not that different from the British middle classes. The rule with the royal summer garden parties is that you may automatically bring any unmarried children you have between the ages of eighteen and twenty-five. However any married children must be asked separately. This is to enable the available posh to swim in the same heated gene pool as the rest of the posh. So, like the Aborigines, if you come from The Belgravia you must marry A Kensington & Chelsea. And your children will go to The Eton, if male, and The Benenden, if female. If you come from The Knightsbridge you must marry into The Army and your children will be called Hannah, Chloë, Sebastian or Charlie. They will marry into The Westminster. And if you come from The North, you're probably asked to a different garden party so that no one runs the risk of you contaminating the posh people.

Despite the centrality of the two particular elements of vows and witnesses, trying to organise a wedding has become very entangled in etiquette, particularly for the middle class. *Debrett's* finds itself quite clear about, for instance, the invitations. They should be 'eight inches by six across. Folded white or cream matt card is most commonly used, and black copperplate engraved script is the preferred typeface. Thermography – shiny black pseudo engraving – is particularly depressing . . .' And among the middle classes, people do indeed surreptitiously run a snooty finger over the typeface of an invitation to see if it's raised and thus engraved. On the basis of which, frankly, they judge whether the wedding is a bit common or sufficiently fashionable. With their neighing voices, this is part of the upper-class bray-dar, designed to spot the presence of intruders. But, honestly: how much of a disaster is it if a wedding invitation is only seven by five and they used the kind of printing that the blind can't read. Can we predict immediate divorce? And, incidentally, Harrods quote the price of engraving at roughly double that of thermography. Hell; if you want to send out invitations that are fifteen inches square with a stuffed heart in pink satin on the front, go ahead. You're in love!

There are an enormous number of rules like that one and *Debrett's* devotes quite some attention to detail about, for instance, the morning coat, the shoes (black leather lace-ups not Gucci loafers), French cuffs and so on in its advice. It does, however, make the classic mistake of assuming that these are the universal signifiers of what it calls 'the traditional church wedding in Britain'. We can say with confidence, however, that this really is limited to one section of the population only. In one sense, it's a class fandango that lives in a world about which *Debrett's* can reliably assume that men will have in their wardrobe a tie that 'can be old school or regiment'. That's not to say that there aren't customs for which people have considerable affection and which have become traditional over the passage of time. Something old, something new, something borrowed, something blue are absolutely traditional values that were linked together into a rhyme as comparatively recently as Victorian times. It ended with the now seldom repeated line 'and a silver sixpence in her shoe'. Each value makes sense: the old symbolises continuity with your life before marriage, the new your future. The borrowed should be something from a happily married couple so that their good fortune spills over into your life together. And blue because it's the colour associated with purity, probably because, for reasons of scarcity until relatively recently, it was the most highly valued pigment and thus the Virgin Mary was painted in blue.

The point is that all these customs are delightful, but they're all adopted and melded in different ways to create conventions around marriage. You only have to look at the hoops through which Prince Charles and Camilla Parker Bowles had to jump in order to make up a marriage ceremony that satisfied Church, state, people and the Queen to realise that even the royal family, in earlier times the very authors of the tablets of stone that came down from etiquette mountain, do not have an absolute standard against which to measure the traditional nature of a wedding. It's infinitely adaptable to circumstance and personal choice. It's an eclectic mix drawn from many sources. The idea of an engagement, for instance, originates from the early habit of stealing a bride. The Anglo-Saxons did it and before them the myth of the rape of Sabine women at the foundation of Rome in 753 BC, perhaps given colour in your imagination by Nicolas Poussin's seventeenth-century depiction of it, helped to create the idea that there should be a period between choosing a bride and actually marrying her. This was intended to give the groom a chance to pay for her, hence her engagement ring, which these days some guides madly recommend should cost the groom a month's salary.

So if instead we are trying to find some principles with which to guide our behaviour around weddings, we might start with the idea that it is a contract made between two people and witnessed and honoured by their family and friends, rather than chafe about the printing of the wedding invitation, the colour of the bride's dress, what the bridegroom wears or who stands where in the receiving line. In essence you simply have to agree to be husband and wife, or partners for life, in front of witnesses. And that, gloriously distilled, is it. There are only four essential, and legal, ingredients in a wedding: a bride and a groom (or two of each in Vermont and soon in Britain), a celebrant and a witness. And in California, with a little planning, you can even register anyone you want as a celebrant for a day. So your wedding doesn't even have to have the semi-official imprimatur of some local government bureaucrat. But essentially the two main things that we have to worry about with weddings are the guests and the vows.

Whom you invite

There is potential for considerable upset with the guest list at a wedding. Firstly, what you can afford will decide the numbers. Money, if you haven't got that much, will limit the guests and, even if you have loads, Westminster Abbey is still only so big. If the ceremony is a balance between the couple and their families, the guest list has to balance who the two of you want to invite with those your parents want to invite. Some weddings are more significant as family events and others focus almost entirely on the couple. Typically, younger and first-time couples have more involvement from their parents and, obviously, if you're a bit longer in the tooth and been and done it before you're more likely to take charge. To be frank, it probably depends on the nature of the relationship you have with your parents. But if the point of a wedding is to meld two individuals, two families and two groups of friends then negotiations need to take place.

If manners are about the ability to pass around

potentially hazardous slaloms, they would dictate that both sides try to minimise any conflict.

Relatives are an occupational hazard of getting married. Blame anthropology. If you want total control, perhaps the best thing to do is not get married and just move in together and have a party. But if you get married there'll be relatives. There are only three times in your life when you get kissed by old women, to whom you are related, who have a mole with a heat-seeking strand of stealth hair that pricks your cheek: birth, marriage and your funeral. And at one of them, you're dead. Which is a relief. But at weddings you might find that you have relatives you've never heard of. Under the pressure of duty from your parents you might be forced to invite all kinds of relations, from distant cousins to step-goduncles. (I went to a wedding where a friend of mine actually had one of those.) When who you really want to ask are your friends. You can fight or you can compromise. In the end there's a balance between family and self. You can also use the A list, B list system, but that has to be handled with a certain diplomatic adroitness. With this method there are those who get invited to everything, others who get invited to the reception, and yet others who get invited only to the party in the evening. And my fantasy is that there are some who are invited just to press their noses up against the window of the wedding feast, like

Tiny Tim, and peer in through the frosted glass at everybody else having a good time. This last is the American Presidential Inauguration system. There are actually people who are sent invitations and then a week or so later they get a card telling them they're not expected to accept. Talk about a frock teaser.

Guests are the people who stand guarantor to your vows. In the Christian tradition this practice declined quite disastrously at one stage. You know things are going badly when someone has to legislate to make it happen. There was such a rise in clandestine marriages that at the Council of Trent in 1545–63 two things were made Church law – the reading of the banns of marriage, which publicised the couple's intentions, and the stipulation that a marriage could only be carried out by a priest with at least two witnesses. Not everybody observes this. One of my oldest friends got married in his lunch hour and the witness was a man in City Hall in Santa Monica. And Britney Spears' lightning wedding was witnessed by the bellhop from the hotel where it took place, the Palms Casino in Las Vegas.

My friend is ten years in. Britney quit after two days. But witnesses are there to stand surety for you, to stand guarantor for the vows you make. So the invitation list must fan out from those who are most important to you to witness your wedding. You will be pushed and pulled, by family mainly, to include people out of duty. Well, if there's room fine, but don't let Great Aunt Matilda, whom you haven't seen since you were in nappies, stake a higher claim than your closest friend who, if things get tough, will be there to support you. But, equally, you have to acknowledge the importance of a wedding for your families. And thus begin the endless rounds of compromise and discussion. Sorry not to be definitive, but manners will be about how you resolve those disputes as much as they will help you decide who is on the guest list.

And for guests their duty is to honour the couple. In all the different forms of dress at all of the different kinds of weddings, one things stands out. People make an effort, whether it's the morning dress uniform of the *Four Weddings* brigade, the blue suit in the pub or the silk and satin saris of a Hindu wedding in the Borough of Brent: people are wearing their best at a celebration in which they play the part of sincerity.

The vows

Couples now get married in town halls, palaces, football grounds, on the beach, in hotels, in casinos, and weddingvenues.com lists just over three thousand venues in thirty-eight categories, including an island, a folly, five zoos, four quarries, an abbey and nine radio studios. The background to people's wedding photos has changed dramatically since, in April 1995, the places approved for marriage were broadened by law from just churches and register offices. However, the centrepiece of the ceremony, the vows of marriage, have still to contain certain key words. In England and Wales if you don't say, 'I do solemnly declare that I know not of any lawful impediment why I . . . [your name] . . . may not be joined in matrimony to . . . [your partner's name]' and they are followed with what are called the contracting words, 'I call upon these persons here present to witness that I . . . [your name again] . . . do take thee . . . [your partner's name] . . . to be my lawful wedded husband [or wife]', then you aren't married. In France you have to say your vows in front of the mayor. The French are *très* sticky about this. If you don't get married by the mayor in the mayor's office, you aren't married. And that's it. It's been like that since Napoleon and it looks like it'll go on being like that until Josephine finally gets a kiss.

But once you've satisfied the law – secular or religious – the world of vows is, in that curious molluscular phrase, your oyster. And boy, do people take advantage of that. There are hundreds of tool kits on the web. Oh yes. For $17 only, you can learn to string together a series of meaningless clichés that could, as far as I can see, describe any relationship from Sooty and Sweep's to Rhett Butler and Scarlett O'Hara's. So to avoid you having to pay the money, here's an all-purpose one that I cobbled together using the basic Christian one as its backbone. Short of her promising 'to always get in the truck' and him 'to always put the toilet seat down', as was solemnly vowed in a recent Mississippi wedding, this encompasses most eventualities:

I [bride/groom], take you [groom/bride], to be my [wife/husband/partner], my constant friend, my love, my darling, my beloved, my sweetheart, my fancy one, my sweetie, my sugar, my honey bunch, my precious one, my jewel, my flower, my mopsy, my moppet, my popsy, my poppet, my petkins, my lamb, my precious, my dear, to have and to hold from this day forward, for better or for worse, for richer, for poorer, in sickness and in health, in good times and in bad, and in joy as well as in sorrow, in times of plenty and in times of want, in times of failure and in times of triumph, when the day smiles, when the day frowns, when the horses lose, when the geegees come in, when fat, when slim, with bad breath, a hangover, and the taste of forty Silk Cut on my tongue . . . [add at will] to love and to cherish, to nurture you, and to grow with you, trust you and respect you, laugh with you and cry with you, loving you faithfully regardless of the obstacles we may face together, I eagerly anticipate the chance to grow together, getting to know the (man/woman) you will become, and falling in love a little more every day, but to go to therapy when it goes wrong and mediation when we fall apart, from this day forward until death do us part.

Does that cover everything?

The point is, though, to make the vows that honour your relationship. Not many women include obey any longer and many people start with the Church of England standard set because, if nothing else, they have the comfort of familiarity, not least thanks to Johnny Speight and Alf Garnett: 'For better, for worse, for richer, for poorer, in sickness and in health, to love and to cherish, till death us do part.' I have seen someone on their third marriage promise that again. And I have seen people on the first hesitate to commit. Vows are heady stuff. They are the contract of fidelity. If marriages, and commitments, are a key building block of society then the best one can say is that couples must make vows that they know they can keep, although one can't help smiling at both the bad fortune and good intentions that flowed from the vows of the labourer who was convicted in 1845 of bigamy. Reported on the Jane Austen website, The Republic of Pemberley, Mr Justice Maule in his judgement said:

Prisoner at the bar, you have been convicted before me of what the law regards as a very grave and serious offence: that of going through the marriage ceremony a second time while your wife was still alive. You plead in mitigation of your conduct that she was given to dissipation and drunkenness, that she proved herself a curse to your household while she remained mistress of it, and that she had latterly deserted you; but I am not permitted to recognise any such plea. You had entered into a solemn arrangement to take her for better, for worse, and if you infinitely got more of the latter, as you appear to have done, it was your duty patiently to submit. You say you took another person to become your wife because you were left with several young children . . . but the law makes no allowance for bigamists with large families. Had you taken the other female to live with you as a concubine, you would never have been interfered with by the law. But your crime consists in having – to use your own language – preferred to make an honest woman of her.

But the judge's compassion showed through in the sentence 'It is my duty to pass upon you such sentence as I think your offence deserves, and that sentence is, that you be imprisoned for one day; and in as much as the present assizes are three days old, the result is that you will be immediately discharged.'

Be full of care with vows.

FUNERALS

And now to turn to the other moment, the second rite of passage.

There used to be a shop in Brighton called Occasionally Christmas. Very annoying really. There is nothing occasional about Christmas whatsoever. It comes around once a year with fantastically predictable regularity. While death isn't exactly accurately foreseeable, it is nonetheless a dead certainty. Yet in British culture we tend to treat it when it happens as if it's a terrible surprise, mainly because we've failed to talk about it in advance. Then when we do talk about it we cover it with a blanket sense of denial enhanced with a very broad palette of euphemisms. The dead person becomes 'the deceased' or 'the loved one'. Corpses – there's a word you're never supposed to use outside the dissecting room – are put in 'caskets', rather than coffins and 'prepared' rather than embalmed. Determined not to inhabit this world of circumlocution, when my mother died I asked a friend to give my apologies for a meeting that I was supposed to chair. I also asked her if she would explain the reason. She did. Apparently very straightforwardly. But several days later one of the other people who had been there said to me, hardly moving his lips in an expression of profound discretion, 'I hear you've had a bit of family trouble'. I almost laughed out loud as a garden fence over which he now appeared to be discussing intimate genito-urinary problems seemed to spring up between us. 'No,' I said, 'no family trouble. My mother died. But no family trouble.' I am afraid he started at the word 'died' as if I'd slapped him.

Death is most confusing to us. At funerals, where we are probably experiencing the maximum sadness we are expected to display the minimum emotion. It's very British. Prince William and Prince Harry were unanimously praised, and with much justification, for keeping astonishing composure as they followed Princess Diana's coffin through London. Their control there, and on the walkabouts they made as much to console themselves, one suspects, as to meet The People, was so distinct from the wailing and weeping of some in the crowd – who knew her only through *Hello!* magazine and the endless front-page images taken by the paparazzi – as the cortège passed. There was, to borrow a waspish phrase from the film critic

Leslie Halliwell in *Halliwell's Filmgoer's Companion* on the death of James Dean, 'an astonishing worldwide outburst of emotional necrophilia'. This admiration for restraint is at the heart of our conflicting attitude towards ritual in Britain, and particularly around death. We're wary of the emotion of it. We're very good at ceremony as long as it involves the military, lots of uniforms, probably horses, certainly a band and the presence of at least some very senior politicians or, if it's a very smart event, some royals. We are less sure of ourselves when there is no band, no pomp and just us, the people we love and that aching void left by the dead, which the vicar at the funeral of my mother, a large woman in every sense of the word, described as 'an Audrey-shaped space'.

If the purpose of manners is to ease our passage through situations pregnant with the possibility for hostility, fear, chaos and lack of control, then funerals will be a very good place to have some. If they are there to guide us predictably in situations where our temper, our tears or our awkwardness are in danger of flying out of control then they are the safety net beneath us as we walk the tightrope of social engagement with people whom we don't always know, or know anything about, in situations where we feel unsure. Funerals and their rituals embody the contradiction between our emotions and what we see as some kind of self-preservation. It's common to mock restraint, to hold up Oprah and Trisha, the twin transatlantic TV goddesses of emotional evacuation, and praise all things unrestrained in a culture where the commonplace is that we 'deal with issues' by talking about them. 'Sharing.' The formal rituals of death, however, are only part of the way we deal with the howling grief. And some people, many people, find solace and calm in the formality, which gives significance to their actions at a funeral. 'Where words are inadequate have a ritual' goes an old anonymous saying. We are conflicted in all of this because we don't necessarily want to conform to rigid rules in mourning. We don't want to be told what to do, what to wear, what to sing and what to say. Nor, equally, do we want to be thrown on to the tempest-tossed waves of our emotions to survive without a safety rail. We want to navigate the way through what can be agonising times knowing that there is somewhere to seek refuge from the endless churning of grief. We want to be able to volunteer for formality, when we need it. But also to be supported and under-stood when we want to howl to the wind. Frankly it's a minefield. And full of surprises.

After my father's funeral, I left the church and walked into the brilliant December sunshine. Outside the porch stood his three greatest friends. They had lost their D'Artagnan. Or their Porthos or their Aramis. Or the one whose name no one can ever remember. Oh, yes. Athos. And they looked as if they were five years old in their loss, these men of sixty-seven, who had fought together through the shuddering experience of the Second World War. They could barely speak. I could only look behind their eyes to hear what they wanted to say and only hope that they could see my feelings too. Formality saved us. After what they'd been through together, what did they want to share tears with a twenty-eight-year-old for? So we shook hands, patted each other's elbows. Did all those splendidly manly things, which were strangely comforting. And, of course, then went to lunch. There my godfather, another military man, a general with a badger moustache, black one side, white on the other, caused by a shrapnel hit in the same war, was in tremendous form. 'What day did he actually die on?' he barked. I told him. 'Good God, I thought so. That was the same day he was wounded in the war, you know.' He paused. Smiled. And then, 'Not a very good day for him really, was it?' I hooted and dropped my glass. And these military men laughed with such relief at the badger's cocked snook at propriety that they felt momentarily whole again.

The advance of medical technology, the development of disease inhibitors like vaccination and treatments that prolong life, have made our attitudes to the rituals of death rather different from those who lived before. And markedly different, possibly, from those who still in this century live denied those advances and so suffer the outrages of often preventable slaughter by war or disease. Those in Britain who lived and died in centuries past without the benefit of water-borne public sanitation experienced death as a far earlier and more brutal consequence of birth than we can ever imagine. Today death is more often moved further down the chronology of our lives towards Jaques' 'second childishness and mere oblivion, sans teeth, sans eyes, sans taste, sans everything'. Which, with the NHS providing at least spectacles and dentistry these days, has been a tiny bit alleviated since Shakespeare's time. Most of us now die in old age. According to the Office of National Statistics life expectancy in Britain for men is around seventy-five and for women over eighty and it has risen dramatically in the last twenty-five years. So we are even more shocked by the death of a child than perhaps people were in the past. But despite all this we nonetheless don't seem quite yet to have adjusted to the inevitability of the unavoidable consequence of old age. You see, you can find many, many ways of avoiding saying it. But here it is: at the end of your life you die. And unless you're religious, that's it. And it is simply not bad manners to mention this. It is just worth thinking about exactly how you do it.

In the past in Britain, people for the most part dealt with the process of dying in the context of a far more enthusiastic and near universal embrace of religion. Child mortality and sweeping epidemics of disease, from the first bubonic plague which raged in Rome for half a century from 540, to influenza and typhoid, smallpox, dysentery, malaria, measles and yellow fever wiped out millions. But so much of the reaction to this decimation in the past depended on people's attitudes towards God. For instance, if you were Puritan, death was just God's punishment for life's sinfulness, so rather depressingly there was little that either you or your friends could do on your deathbed. Praying wouldn't alter your fate. The University of Houston's Digital History site records that of the original 102 Pilgrims who landed in Plymouth in 1620 half of them were dead by the other side of the first winter. It was said that so many people died among the first wave of pioneers in America that the pealing of church bells at funerals was outlawed because it had become a public nuisance. Instead, gloves were sent out to relatives and friends to invite them to a funeral. Andrew Eliot, the minister at Boston's North Church, collected three thousand pairs in thirty-two years.

To a Catholic, however, praying was thoroughly

worthwhile. As was confession since, as a priest recently said to me, 'Being a Catholic is rather like having a pay-as-you-go phone. You use up credit. Then you just get some more.' On your deathbed you charge up your account for Heaven with a hearty confession and hope that God will let you talk and then judge you kindly.

If you were a Roman you believed a modified version of the Hellenic myth of the afterlife and the underworld. Hermes (Mercury in Latin) took dead souls to the River Styx where they paid Charon, the ferryman, to take them across. They had to pass Cerberus, the three-headed dog that in pictures on the side of urns curiously always looks a little like Barbara Woodhouse, to be judged by Minos, Aeacus and Rhadamanthus and they then spend eternity in either Elysium or the Plain of Asphodel, which were ruled over by Hades.

The point of this historical excursion is not to prepare you for the next pub quiz, but to make the point that the rituals of death are generally divided into those that are meant for the person who's died and to ease their passage to the afterlife and those that are there to comfort the living. The Aztecs, who, as we shall see in the chapter on table manners, had an extremely unhealthy obsession with death, had a number of the former. They had a god of the underworld called Mictlantecuhtli, who always carried a snake, a sceptre and a shield. One appalling ritual he required, for instance, was that, when a lord died, a slave had to be sacrificed to accompany him and help him in the afterlife. And the lord's wife was also buried in order to serve her husband. Amazing that a man can't boil an egg or do his own washing even in the beyond. But there you are.

To Mexicans death was not an altogether terrible idea; it was simply a point on the continuity between this life and the next. And, unlike in Western religions, it was the way you'd died rather than how you'd behaved in life that determined the kind of funeral you got and the destiny of your soul. So if you died in childbirth you were buried not cremated. If you died of any number of diseases like gout, scabies or leprosy you were said to go to a terrestrial paradise called Tlalocan, the home of the god Tlaloc, which was wonderfully fertile and full of flowers. And so on.

The Chinese perm a combination of your manner of death and your status in life to determine what kind of funeral you get. The rituals are both for the dead and for those left behind. And whatever the funeral, all the statues of deities in the home must be covered with red paper, so they don't see the coffin or corpse, and all mirrors must be turned to the wall because the myth has it that a person who sees the reflection of a coffin in the mirror will have a death in their household soon. There is a particular strictness about the colours of clothes worn by the different mourners. Children and daughters-in-law should wear black, because they grieve the most, grandchildren blue and great-grandchildren light blue. Sons-in-law wear brighter colours, such as white, as they are considered outsiders. The children and daughters-in-law also wear a hood of sackcloth over their heads.

All around the world one can go relating customs from different traditions and cultures, but wherever you look, the formalities are designed either to speed the dead on to the afterlife or to give a channel for grief, never mind how restrained, in the British case, or full of wailing and crying, as is the custom with Chinese blood relatives. A remarkably eloquent pair of examples of managing grief come from two Maori tangis – the practice of people gathering around the body from the moment of death until the funeral – which were recorded by a Homedeath Support Group in Palmerston North, New Zealand, a couple of years ago. At one, a daughter owed money by her mother when she died apparently stood by the coffin and shouted, 'You bloody bitch, what about that fifty dollars you still owe me? . . . I'll never get that now . . . You better have it when I get to see you, when I get up there.' We British are tut-tutting already. And at another a woman, angered by her father's suicide, yelled and shouted and shook the coffin. Neither woman was restrained by the others at the tangi, but they were watched over in their grief, accompanied in their temporary madness. And the ritual gave a kind of safety to their complete lack of control. What rituals do supremely well is to generate social support.

On the Festival of Quingming, China's traditional day for sweeping the graves and remembering the dead, a couple of years ago more than 1.1 million people took the subway in Bejiing alone to visit the graves of their relatives where they burned paper money and feasted. Honouring the dead like this is such a mass pursuit in China that in 1956 Mao drew up plans to outlaw it. The Communist Party regarded it as a bourgeois reliance on superstition. But he was never able to enact the laws. And it has become such a huge feast now that, in an attempt to stop people using so much land for burial, and creating waste and pollution with the burning ceremonies, the Chinese government has set up and funded an online cemetery called Earth Village in the hope that people will now choose cremation rather than burial and mourn their relatives via the internet rather than in person by the grave. Sure. That's going to happen. thebereaved@theafterlife.cn Subject heading: still thinking of you. cc: the family. Click here to burn paper money.

Grief is not private. We learn to share it and respect it. Even the extraordinarily elaborate, and apparently entirely oppressive, rules for widows' mourning clothes in Victorian England, whose middle classes had an obsession with the rituals of death, had a greater social purpose. Wearing official mourning was a way to indicate that a person was not to be expected to engage fully socially for a period of time. In a way it was protection for them, although the rules did become preposterous in their complexity by the end of Victoria's reign. *Collier's Cyclopedia*, published in 1901, devoted more than three and a half thousand words, in ludicrous detail, to the twelve months of a widow's first mourning and the twelve months of her second, when, you'll be glad to know, things relaxed just a little. In the second twelve months she didn't have to wear a cap any longer. Yippee! Freedom at last! The chapter went on and on about the materials for dresses (rainproof crape with a mentale of silk or Henrietta), caps in tulle with streamers (and instructions on how to make them at home), the appropriate jewellery (anything in jet) and even the right knickers, which in the context seems a little bit unnecessary as presumably the poor old widow wasn't supposed be thinking about anyone else seeing her in her knickers.

Much has been written by feminists asking why widows have to suffer so much when their husbands die – in many cultures, not just Victorian England – but why, when their wives die, men just go back to the bride shop and get a new one. Usually younger. But setting that aside for a moment, in the Victorian case what looks like an inordinate display, boasting almost, of grief was in fact mainly a useful warning to others. It was a public sign, a caution to tread carefully around the bereaved and to treat them gently for a considerable amount of time. This rigmarole of Victoriana, as curious and as much an indicator of class as it sounds to us now, does direct us towards the most difficult questions we have about how to deal with mourning. Is grief private? How long does it go on? And what is the best reaction of those around the grieving? Each of those questions rears its head during three phases of the process of dying and mourning.

The dying

Curiously, as I write now, someone has just phoned to tell me that a friend – not a close friend but someone I work with – is sitting by his partner's bed as she goes through what everybody thinks will be her last days.

What to do when you receive such news? Phone?

No, obviously not unless you know them very well. The purpose of manners in this situation is primarily to help them through it. To phone means to talk and unless they know you equally as well, it is a burden to have to explain what is happening, probably all over again after the last call. The minutiae of death are endless. How was she responding last night? Was she calm? Is she awake? What do the doctors say? What are they prescribing? Is she eating? Can you talk to each other? It's as if we ask the questions in order to occupy ourselves. The chatter fills the space where otherwise there would be a danger of silence or tears. We know what is happening. But you think there is always a chance. No, there isn't. Not usually with cancer and potentially fatal diseases. Good manners means going with the truth. Don't pretend it's all la-la-la and fine. Nothing helps people facing loss and grief less than denial. But telling the truth doesn't mean speaking it all. It can mean managing it. The best you can do with someone whom you don't know well is to make sure that, via someone who does know them well, they know you are thinking of them. Or alternatively e-mails are great in this situation because you can send them often, they can be brief and the person can respond or not, depending on their mood. It's just a way of letting them know that you know.

The dynamic is different when you are close to the

person dying, when you are involved in the death. When a very dear and voluble but nonetheless only subtly emotional friend was dying of cancer, all his friends were concerned about whether or not he wanted to talk about the fact that he was dying. Whether he was afraid. What he thought lay in wait for him, if anything. In a sense should we be Puritans or Catholics? Was there nothing to do or did he want to, if not confess, at least sift through his life? He was of the Queen Mary – a woman famously composed and tight-lipped about her feelings – school of emotions. You learned to read the signs. A pat on the shoulder from him meant close friendship, thanks for being here, even an acknowledgement of love between mates. An ironic raising of the eyebrow could write paragraphs about how he had been very hurt by something but had got over it now. A man of emotional runes. So the prospect of asking him whether he was frightened of dying ran the danger of trespass. So the subject was approached crab-like, the guiding principle being the rather obvious one that it should be him who determined the limits of the conversation. There is no obligation to talk about what you fear most in the world. It doesn't always help and, yes, manners means following their lead when it's them doing the dying, not mimicking the dictates of sofa TV and amateur psychology to share, to get it out in the open.

So a conversation was carefully embarked upon. 'Was he getting enough information from the doctors?' 'Yes.' 'Was it the information that he wanted? Were they being as clear to him as he wanted them to be?' 'Yes.' Pause. 'They skirt around it all tho'.' Conan the Barbarian would have understood what he meant. 'Would you like them not to? Would you like them to go further?' Longer pause. 'No. It's about all that I can cope with for the moment.' The opportunity was opened and the line was drawn. He never did say what he feared. Or whether in the end he was at peace. That was his decision.

Other people in the last weeks of illness, of course, sit in bed and hold court with their friends while they, metaphorically or literally, brandish their turban to show their chemo baldness. They set an ordered pace with their goodbyes. They organise everything and probably have little truck with what they regard as squeamishness on the part of those they are leaving behind. One person I knew, who has since died of brain cancer, wouldn't see certain people whom she regarded as a drain because all they wanted to do was sit and be sad and cry and generally be a drag and indulge their own emotions. She wanted to be the centre of attention. She wanted to experience her death, not their anxieties, she used to say. With people who choose this way of dying, whatever their fear of death or their peace with it, they live it out through their form of control. Manners with them, just as it is with the emotionally more subterranean, is to take their lead, whatever it is, and follow it.

It's not rude to raise death in polite conversation. It may also not be rude sometimes to ignore it. The most difficult thing is that we feel awkward about it. The people we know are going to die are the terminally ill, the very old and our parents. Ease their path towards it, if you can. Countenancing your parents' death is almost impossible; it makes you both an orphan, which makes you feel like a child, and the next generation, which makes you feel like a grown-up. Good manners, that which in this case manages the hurt and sadness between us, requires that we follow the desires of the dying and afterwards respect the wishes of the bereaved. Our language in Britain doesn't particularly help us to deal with it openly, though. When my father died, people kept on referring to him euphemistically as 'your late father' and I kept on thinking 'Late? He's not late. He's never going to show up.'

•

Making the announcement and how to react

There is a terribly cruel joke, which I heard when I was a child. It's cruel enough for me to blush when telling it. But it's not cruel enough to stop me. The parade ground. A soldier's mother has died and the sergeant major is instructed by the, inevitably chinless and rather wet superior officer to pass on the sad news. So at parade the sergeant major lines the troops up. 'At ease.' They stand easy. And then he barks, bold as brass, 'Corporal Smith.' Smith steps forward. 'Your mother is DEAD.' The poor corporal faints with shock and grief. The officer calls the sergeant major in and tears him off a strip for his appalling insensitivity. 'For God's sake, man, be a little more subtle.' A month later, Corporal Smith's father dies – in the way of jokes and fortunately not so often in life. The sergeant major lines the troops up. 'At ease.' And barks (again, I imagine, as bold as brass), 'Everyone whose father is alive, take one step forward. Corporal Smith, where the hell do you think you're going?'

Sorry.

But there is a good way and a bad way to impart terrible news. The formal announcement in the papers is what the middle classes do. They cost a fortune, but socially you're simply not dead, my dear, until they've announced it in *The Times*. But whether it's the newspaper you read, a letter you open, a phone call you get or a bit of news in the supermarket, it's shocking, or just sad, or surprising, or upsetting to hear that somebody you like has died. The messenger is immaterial. E-mail is a huge help. In preventing people whom you want to tell personally from hearing by accident, the speed of the ether is wonderful. And by telling people you are inviting them to share in your grief. Recently someone I know sent an e-mail to all her friends the day after her mother died in which she'd written a short yet remarkably true portrait of her mum. The cc list made her friends feel part of a gang, there to remember, mourn and help.

The most difficult question for us is: how to help? How to react? And whether the death is expected and quiet or unexpected and appalling, like a violent suicide or a fatal accident, the difficulty of knowing what to do is still there; it's just really a matter of degree. There's a sort of helplessness. 'I never know what to say,' people flounder, sometimes adding a joke. 'No point in saying "sorry". I mean, it's not my fault they died.' A weak smile. One of the most famous examples, recently brought back into people's consciousness by Steven Spielberg who quoted it in *Saving Private Ryan*, is Abraham Lincoln's letter to a Mrs Lydia Bixby, who, he believed, had lost five sons in the Civil War: 'I feel how weak and fruitless must be any words of mine which should attempt to beguile you from the grief of a loss so overwhelming,' he wrote. There's a kind of comfort, and a great poignancy, in knowing that the man who wasn't quite lost for words at the Gettysburg Address had an almost overwhelming lump in his throat at the thought of the death of a group of unknown young soldier brothers. However, it's all very well to take the trouble to write to someone but, to be honest it's not that much help to moan on about not knowing what to say. Brilliantly though Lincoln, and you, might phrase it.

So what to write? *Debrett's* takes the formal, stiff-lipped approach to condolence: 'Sorrow is sacred and to intrude on private grief remains bad manners.' Nonsense. It does at least suggest that you should write but doesn't go much further than suggesting that you don't bother with black-edged notepaper and adds a slightly unnecessary warning not to use 'jolly coloured stationery'. Well, thanks. Manners, if they confirm the bonds between us, require that we don't back off when it all gets a bit messy. Stay away when there's tears, darling; you may get your social life damp. Grief is not popular or particularly welcome. But it's terribly common. As the Victorians used to say rather dolefully, again quoted in *Collier's Cyclopedia*, 'Who breathes must suffer, and who thinks must mourn.' In the fact that every one of us will feel immeasurable loss and consequent grief one day lies the clue as to how we should react when others are going through it. Manners require that we do more than churn out a standard letter. 'My heartfelt condolences to you on your loss.' How heartfelt is that? It sounds more like an Out-of-Office AutoReply on e-mail. You might as well address the envelope to Occupant and the letter To Whom It May Concern. Or, as Donald Rumsfeld did in the first Christmas of the Iraq War in 2004, why not just have letters to the bereaved signed by machine. As the widow of one of the soldiers who died pointed out rather sharply, 'The soldiers out there aren't machines, *they*'re human beings.' Quite. Letters of condolence should not be written by rote. Manners dictate, rather, that they should summon up the singularity of a friendship and try and pay tribute to the absolute uniqueness of each relationship.

If you don't know the person who died but rather the person who survives, then the point of the letter is to tell them that you, another human being, understand their grief. Simply that you know what it is like to feel loss. Not their loss. You can't know that. But you can know the universal feeling of distress.

After some time of estrangement from each other, Thomas Jefferson, no slouch with words when he composed the Declaration of Independence, wrote to his predecessor as President of the United States, John Adams, on 13 November 1818 after the death of his wife. It is a beautiful letter of condolence that you can reread endlessly and still feel comforted anew. Jefferson manages to summon up Adams's loss with an appeal to the sadnesses in his own life, yet in a way that is so modest it doesn't substitute his own grief for Adams's.

> The public papers, my dear friend, announce the fatal event of which your letter of Oct. 20 had given me ominous foreboding. Tried, myself, in the school of affliction, by the loss of every form of connection which can rive the human heart, I know well and feel what you have lost, what you have suffered, are suffering, and have yet to endure. The same trials have taught me that for ills so immeasurable, time and silence are the only medicines. I will not, therefore, by useless condolences, open afresh the sluices of your grief, nor, although mingling sincerely my tears with yours, will I say a word more where words are vain, but that it is of some comfort to us both that the term is not very distant at which we are to deposit in the same cerement our sorrows and suffering bodies, and to ascend in essence to an ecstatic meeting with the friends we have loved and lost, and whom we shall still love and never lose again. God bless you and support you under your heavy affliction.

If you did know the person who has died well, then a letter's best intent is to try and summon up their spirit. Adjectives, stories, anything, no matter how small, that makes them appear again. In writing you are, through memory, filling a small amount of the void left in the life of someone bereaved. Any way you remember the one who's died, just put it down and send it off. The echo of them when they were alive will be good comfort to the person left behind and confirm your friendship with them.

One more story. When the theatre critic Jack Tinker, himself to die prematurely before he was sixty, lost his daughter Charlotte aged only twenty-four, he was stunned by grief. His great newspaper friend, the astrologer Patric Walker, he told me, made a quiet and immensely kind gesture. He sent him an open air ticket to Greece, where the rewards of telling people that if they were Capricorn they were most compatible with Scorpio and that the colour blue was lucky for them today, had bought him a villa. Jack eventually, after months, got on a plane. For two weeks he sat in the sun. Patric never once asked him about his daughter. When Jack was ready, one night right at the end of his stay, they talked for hours. And Patric said, as the sun was rising: 'Don't look on it as a life interrupted. Try to think of it as a life completed and then you can take it with you for the rest of your life.'

I plead guilty to having repeated that to a number of people a number of times over the years.

A final golden rule. Never text a condolence. Your jaw may have dropped at the very thought. Surely not? But, yes, a friend of mine whose father died received just such a message. 'sry yr fther ded. hope ur ok.' Well, it was longer than that. But, be a love; never do it. It doesn't quite give the impression that you actually care.

Ceremonies

The formality of funerals and memorial services has dissolved over recent years. We watch the Remembrance Day parades year after year and the sight of the very old miraculously still standing remains as moving as ever as their numbers dwindle. The D-Day celebrations in 2004 were greeted with some nostalgia, those of younger generations moved by the straightness of the veterans' backs and the discipline of their bearing as they honoured their fallen comrades for the last time in public according to their well-worn military traditions. As the war generations die, funerals have started to take on a diversity, which prompted one vicar to remark recently that they were now an opportunity for what he called 'creative grieving'. It's an expressive phrase which certainly guides us well, never mind that it unfortunately sounds much too much like a short course at some dreary college in Cheam.

The various faiths dictate very clearly their particular rules for funerals and committals but, apart from strict religious observance, the vicar's phrase is increasingly true. There is a general acceptance that a funeral's purpose is to reflect the person who has died in the way that those closest, who haven't, decide. In public this was reflected as we watched the modulating of tradition at the funeral of Diana, Princess of Wales. There were moments of sheer horror for some people, uneasy at the mawkishness of Elton John's rewrite of 'Candle In The Wind'. But others were grateful for an opportunity to be part of what they felt was a reclaiming of tradition, an unbending of the stiff backs of the royal family in response to popular demand. And it was, in that dreadful phrase, 'what she would have wanted'. Well, what she would have wanted, like all of us, was to live a long and healthy life, but setting that aside what you want at your funeral is for it to feel like you. And out with the demands of religious observance there is nothing to prevent this idea developing. It has been heavily influenced in the last twenty years or so by both the decline in organised religion and a generation decimated by AIDS. For the first time since the Second World War whole groups of young people have experienced the battering of constant death. Of friends dropping out of life at an alarming rate, far too early. Of current address books still full of names of people who no longer brighten their lives. So the ceremonies bent to the subculture. Drag queens took torch songs and sang them in churches. People read from texts that were both spiritual and profane in memory of people who were often remembered as more gloriously profane than spiritual. Funerals became a pick and mix of tradition, tack and tone.

This has spread to the wider population and has continued to dictate the music, the words, the way we dress at funerals and even the coffins people choose. Barbara Cartland instructed that she should be buried in a cardboard coffin in order to save trees. Although not wishing to trample on any of her family's feelings, one does ponder whether if she had really wanted to save the trees she could have written slightly fewer books. Recently I went to a funeral where a woman who was particularly environmentally aware was cremated in a pink eco-pod. And as with coffins, it's no longer the case that bright clothes are not necessarily worn. Basil once complimented the Major in *Fawlty Towers* for looking particularly smart. And when told that he was going to a funeral Fawlty pointed out that his tie was a bit loud. But the Major just blithely informed Basil that he didn't like the chap. It really is no longer the case that you have to wear black. What to wear is a decision guided by the person who's died. You wouldn't wear the same to a state funeral as you would to the funeral of an AIDS activist in New York. If you were a man, to the former you'd wear morning dress and to the latter probably just a dress. Honour the person in the box.

A generation of people largely untouched by AIDS has reaped the harvest of this, although often the completely free expression of their desires is muffled by grief, and people still frequently opt for the safety of tradition, even if a newer one. Unfortunately at the moment this seems to involve too much Celine Dion and too little decent music. The last time anyone counted, according to the Co-Op Funeral Service the following was the Top 10 of funeral tunes:

1. 'Wind Beneath My Wings' – Bette Midler
2. 'My Heart Will Go On' – Celine Dion
3. 'I Will Always Love You' – Whitney Houston
4. 'The Best' – Tina Turner
5. 'Angels' – Robbie Williams
6. 'You'll Never Walk Alone' – Gerry And The Pacemakers
7. 'Candle In The Wind' – Elton John
8. 'Unchained Melody' – The Righteous Brothers

9. 'Bridge Over Troubled Water' – Simon & Garfunkel
10. 'Time To Say Goodbye' – Sarah Brightman

Canon John Hester, a friend of Peter Sellers, was given a tape by the actor some years before he died with the instructions that it be played only when the coffin was at the church door. Until then it was to remain a secret. The coffin arrived and the canon pushed the 'play' button. The former Goon's coffin was borne down the aisle to the accompaniment of 'In The Mood' by Glenn Miller. Another great figure in entertainment, although nothing like as well known, the anarchic comedian Malcolm Hardy's coffin left the church recently to Elvis Presley's 'Return To Sender'.

While some of you might be shuddering, and others roaring with laughter and thinking how appropriate, the purpose of the funeral is not to prove how smart or culturally upmarket we are; it's to give us a vehicle for our grief and to remember the dead and speed them to whatever afterlife they believed in. And you can be sure that if anyone plays Celine Dion or Sarah Brightman at my funeral, there will be skid marks across the River Styx as I bolt towards Hades.

—◊—

3

PUBLIC PLACES (ESPECIALLY THE CITY)

Unless we venture into steamy jungles among animal predators, swim in crocodile-infested waters or take part in *Big Brother*, cities are potentially some of the most terrifying places we will ever experience. We talk about the 'urban jungle' and 'City sharks'. We can name the threat. We have metaphors for it. So if there is anywhere that we need manners it's in cities. And if there's anywhere we think there are none, it's in cities. If manners are the system by which we reduce the potential for violence between strangers, a method through which we find a way to live at ease with each other, it's in the centres of London, Paris, New York, Rome and other places on the bottom of posh scent bottles, the other vast urban sprawls in the world, that we need them. And that's precisely where we have the most difficulty enforcing them. In all the other chapters of this book, we're dealing with arenas where – never mind how ghastly we think it's all become, never mind how lawless and simply beyond civilisation we fear it's heading – we have at least some measure of control or enforcement, because we're talking about things that happen on private or semi-private territory: in conversation, at weddings and funerals, at the table, at work or in bed. We may not be omnipotent in any of those places – hands up for either work or bed – but at least there's a fighting chance that we might be able to appeal to reason, or hospitality, or the boss, or the other person under the duvet. On the street at the moment it feels as if there's no such appeal possible, no such regulator of behaviour. We are cast as atomised individuals to the winds, left to put our heads down, mind our own business and get on with what we can before fleeing back home to safety at the end of the day.

Cities are places where we think chaos reigns. Yet when we talk of good manners we use words like 'civility' and 'urbanity' which, of course, have urban roots. As those of you who remember *Kennedy's Latin Primer* (or *Kennedy's Eating Primate*, as it could be altered to with very little difficulty using only a felt-tip and a few of the duller moments of the second half of Mr Kember's double Latin) will know, they are derived from *civis* and *urbs*, the Latin for 'city dweller' and for 'city or town'. At odds with our impression of the city as the source of chaos and violence in our lives, it is precisely in the city that we can learn manners, we can learn to get on with each other, to be urbane and civilised. There is a little rhyme published in 1907 in *A Home Idyll* by the American children's writer J.T. Trowbridge:

Men are polished, through act and speech
Each by each,
As pebbles are smoothed on the rolling beach.

Sorry to quote bad poetry at you, but it makes the point. Although, while it appears that 'politeness' has the same root as *polis*, the Greek word for 'city', that's actually a coincidence. That's not its derivation. Politeness comes from the French word for to 'polish'. It is always a shock when any word associated with the French describes something to do with good manners. But politeness is the result of polishing: it's the smoothness which comes from being 'rubbed up' against each other. So while it's an etymological coincidence, it is precisely the city that demands that we have manners. And precisely the city that could teach them to us by pushing us together, enforcing our contact, celebrating our interaction. And it would just make the day go with a bit of a swing if someone actually bothered to hold the door, say thank you, offer us their seat, omit any four-letter words from the description of our driving, restrain themselves from hurling litter out of the car window, not spit gum on the pavement, not stub their fags out on the road, not barge in front of us at the supermarket, not take seven items to the five or fewer checkout, restrain themselves from thrusting the *Big Issue* at us with menaces, stand up on buses, sit down in theatres, switch off their mobiles while eating, scream less into them while on trains, get their feet off the seats and, before I go completely red in the face, burst a valve, have a heart attack and turn into Victor Meldrew, I am going to have the sense to bring this list to an abrupt halt. But you get the idea. It would just be easier to live if any of that happened, let alone raising our game of life through manners above easy even to pleasant. And whatever the desperate moderation of that word, it would be an advance on the constant confrontation and temper that city-living can be.

But for all that, cities still present us with this dilemma. We love them because they exemplify the freedoms that we have gained financially, sexually, politically, ethnically. Even if we live in the country-side we know that the city represents all of that, even if we don't always want to be part of it. We value the freedom and thus the anonymity of the city yet we hate the roughness and aggression that it seems to foster. We are not generally at ease with each other in the city and we find it difficult to create a bond between one another there. For us to behave well we have to feel that there will be some sanction that matters to us if we don't. Even if it's just the stare of the rest of the bus. And to enforce the rules there has to be some kind of shared authority. To some extent in the past, as we've said, that authority came in different areas of our lives from the Makers, Monarchs and Men. In different ways they were the enforcers. But we have thrown off the widespread social deference to them. And now it's down to us. We will have to take responsibility for the enforcement of manners as our own new authority over ourselves.

Yet currently we seem to have 'outsourced' enforcement, to use a dreadful, but in this rare case a usefully accurate, piece of jargon. A youngish guy said to me at dinner recently in the middle of a very well-mannered but actually ferocious argument about this, that as far as he was concerned as long as he could go about his business and get where he wanted with the minimum of fuss that was all he desired out of the city. He thought I, and people like me, were silly old hippies for wanting us all to be 'nice' to each other, as he parodied my idea of city manners with a curl of his metropolitan lip. What about when it goes wrong, I said? As you go about seamlessly getting what you want, what happens when the city malfunctions and there are no manners? What about the drunken behaviour that colonises the streets on Friday and Saturday nights? Or the needless litter? Or the selfish driving by someone who gridlocks an entire traffic flow by barging into the yellow zigzags? He said, 'The police can deal with that. That's why I pay my taxes.'

The police may deal with criminality but whatever the nostalgia, or our parents' nostalgia, about good old Dixon of Dock Green, he never could get people to open doors for people with parcels, stand up on the bus for the elderly or say thank you for letting you into a stream of traffic. Surely in place of the authority of the Maker, Monarchs and Men we need to grow a sense of a collective good that is sufficiently powerful to enforce respectful behaviour towards each other. Manners are only enforceable if we make that duty towards each other something so strongly acknowledged in society that people are embarrassed not to honour it. For instance we need to challenge people when they bawl into their phones. One man I know while on a train to Sheffield heard a woman shouting so loudly into her mobile as she bought this and charged that that he was able to write down all her bank details and credit card numbers. He then texted her the information with the words 'For God's sake, shut up'. She went ballistic, shouting to find out who had done it, but eventually did indeed shut up and the carriage sank with relief into blissful silence. We have to take the risk that we'll be thought a dreadful busybody in the cause of enforcing decent good manners.

I was on a train last year. It was a short journey, only about six minutes from Brighton, where I live, to Falmer, where the university is. Believe you me, I wouldn't have done this if we had been on a train from Brighton to York, because I decided to question a girl sitting next to me who had her dirty shoes up on the seat opposite. Friends tell me I will eventually be stabbed if I go on like this. But it turned out to be a very eloquent experiment. I used this girl as my little lab rat. I said to her, 'Can I ask you a question?' She said, rather reluctantly, 'Yes.' I said, 'Can you tell me why you think it's okay to put your dirty shoes on the seat opposite?' 'Fuck off!' she said. 'Well,' I said, 'that is certainly a response. But it's not the answer to the question, "Can you tell me why you think it's okay?" etc, etc . . .' She effed again and told me in succession that I was 'old', 'about to die' and 'stupid'. I just continued to ask her the question. Then I added one extra element. I asked her whether she thought she ought to worry about the next person who would sit on the seat and whose clothes might then get dirty. She said,

'No one fucking cares about *me*.' Then she got up. I don't blame her, frankly. I was being stupendously annoying. And she walked off to the door to wait for the train to arrive in the station and, as she did, she muttered under her breath, appealing to the other passengers to agree with her judgement that I was, and I think I'm quoting accurately here, 'a complete twat'. I might quibble with the complete. But she got no votes from any of the other pasengers. By the time she got to the door she was isolated. Which I didn't then feel very good about, to be honest.

I apologised to the other passengers for possibly ruining their journey. But they all started to pitch in: 'Why don't we do that more often?' 'We really should challenge people on their manners', and so on. I became the Busybody On High, The Prima Interferer. In the few minutes that we had to talk about this, one person even mused on whether it would have been wrong of her to put her shoes on the seat if the soles had actually been spotlessly clean. A philosopher presumably. The train was going to a university after all. And, for what it's worth, we decided it wouldn't have been wrong because she wouldn't have been risking harm to anyone else. It wasn't the feet on the seat, it was dirt on the skirt of the next person who sat there that was the problem. I had become Wat and Which Tyler all in one, a pedant leading a peasants' revolt against bad manners. But what she said stuck in my mind. 'No one fucking cares about *me*.' It wasn't a sob story. She didn't look poor or abused or addicted. She was a perfectly ordinary sixteen-year-old girl who just didn't have any sense that she had any linking with the world around her. Manners cannot exist in a situation like that.

However, what appears to be an absence of manners isn't always that. It sometimes just flows from the fact that we are all strangers in cities and so we can't necessarily trust the motives of others. If out of the blue a man starts to talk to a woman, should she trust him? If someone chats to you at the ticket machine, do you hold extra firmly on to your bag, in case their accomplice tries to nick it? If someone approaches you in the street, do you rush on for fear of being asked for money? Maybe they were a tourist who just wanted directions. We are not bad mannered necessarily, just reasonably suspicious of strangers. Try smiling at everyone you pass on the pavement next time you go out into town. Give them a big broad toothy one. Let them see the value of the dental work and watch how they run for cover, cross the street or phone for the Psychiatric Service. It's unnerving because it seems like such a rejection, so typical of the brusqueness of the city. Why doesn't anyone smile back at anyone any longer, you wonder? Where have everyone's manners gone? You try an experiment like that and look what happens. People start thinking about locking you up.

I know we're not baboons, but who can trust a smile when you don't know where it's coming from? When baboons seem to 'smile', what they are actually doing is one of two things. If they roll back their gums and show their teeth, their jaws open and apart from each other, then it's an act of aggression, as baring teeth always is. It's one of the reasons why you should never eat with your mouth open. In an anthropological sense, it's a hostile act to show teeth which are potential weapons and with which you will then, if you're a cave man or pre-knife eater, tear apart the meat. So instead of a cheery greeting, smiling with your teeth bared can to someone else be the anthropological equivalent of Clint Eastwood brandishing a .44 Magnum saying go ahead, make my day. But if the baboon's teeth are together and the lips relaxed, it's a friendly gesture. Then again, if a politician, lawyer or salesman does that, you're entitled to be suspicious. What are they trying to slip under my guard? Why should I trust them? And have they got a baby in their arms? Because then it's doubly dubious. Smiles are ambiguous between strangers. Try smiling at the shop assistant in a supermarket and they'll probably look at you as if you've got a turkey up your jumper.

But now try smiling in the countryside. When you next go on a Sunday walk – one of those hearty country walks that involve corrective rural footwear and clothes that create a total absence of any definable bodily shape – try smiling at everyone coming in the opposite direction. Everyone will smile back at you. In fact, if you have a dog, they'll probably talk to you. With the slightest bit of encouragement they'll turn into a version of those awful people you meet on holiday, inevitably swap numbers with and then regret what you've done becuase you say, 'When you're back, do get in touch.' And they do.

Though country dwellers are supposedly suspicious of strangers, even drivers on country lanes acknowledge each other. Despite the fact that in Yorkshire, and other counties where the transition from stranger to local comes only after fifteen years or so's hard, neighbourly work, they just do it with a twitch of a finger on the steering wheel, the North of England equivalent of a team of American cheerleaders and a tickertape parade. But drivers in the city don't even do that. The only way they acknowledge each other is by swearing and shouting insults or indulging in heavy sarcasm about your and my driving. Which apparently is so much worse than theirs.

None of this happens in the country because, somehow, they're nicer people. Sometimes the same people who wave at you on the walk will scowl at you in the city. But when you're on that walk or driving in the country, there is some sort of community inferred from what you are doing, some kind of invisible bond between people who would otherwise be strangers. It takes a conversation to find what you don't have in common – or perhaps what you do. But for the moment, to be walkers or cyclists is enough to imply a connection. And you do even see it between cyclists in cities, where they bond against the common enemy of white van man and other Mr Toads who threaten life and limb.

What we think we like about the countryside is that everybody knows everybody. It's also what we hate about it. Everybody knows everybody's business so there is no privacy. But it's much easier to be polite to the only six people you meet on a sunny day, in a rose-cottage-clustered village, deep in the heart of rural England where you grow what you eat, cook what you serve from scratch and walk your children to the local school before doing the flowers in the church and taking tea with your elderly neighbour.

But our experience is that it's harder to be well mannered in the city, to be polite when we have to drive for twenty minutes in order to shop in a city supermarket where people appear to have taken their kids for a day out mainly in order to smack them in the baking section. And to do it in our lunch hour. And then to collect the kids from school or organise for someone else to collect the kids from school or completely forget to collect the kids from school. While also managing the aggravations and stresses of work. And to battle with private or public transport at the start and end of the day. Struggling through crowds, wading through litter, fighting through traffic, we curse and swear to ourselves at the city. Some of us oh so very mildly and others of us way too loudly. Manners seem impossible in the rush of modern life. We all think that we just need to get where we're going with the minimum of fuss. This is not the case, of course. Manners have nothing to do with the time they take. We are definitely frenetic in the pace of our lives. But we're actually not working any more hours than we were in the 1960s. We are, though, under different kinds of pressure. Pressure to produce and consume; the pressure of ambition; in an uncertain world where no one's job is guaranteed, where work is now flexible, the pressure to demonstrate that we are better and work harder than the next person, not to earn money but in order to survive. Being told that constant change is something we have to embrace hurls us into insecurity and makes us nervous and stressed. Our manners suffer.

We also further distort the pressure of living with

our need for instant satisfaction. A friend of mine's child recently asked for a biscuit, omitting to add 'please'. His mother said to him, 'What's the magic word?' Without hesitation he replied, 'Now.' We can't wait for anything. To a certain degree we live in a Lottery world where we dream of instant riches. Time is foreshortening. People used to be famous for fifteen minutes. Now they're famous *in* fifteen minutes. In the West we live in a society that is standing in front of the microwave and shouting, 'Hurry.' But, nonetheless, even though time may be money, lack of time, and, incidentally, lack of or conversely the possession of money, is not a reason for bad manners. Rich or poor, you can treat people with respect in a nanosecond if you want to. But cities seem to militate against us doing it as much as we'd like to because of the pressures we feel and the sense that we are all strangers when we meet there, with little in common.

Consistently we British dream of a rural existence. According to a MORI poll in 2000, 84 per cent of people in the UK say they want to live in a small village. But in fact only 4 per cent do. And even when we live in a town we recreate the pastoral. In a trice in Fulham and Battersea, seconds after they have bought the house, the middle classes set to and knock through the two front rooms, fill the space with natural wood, Laura Ashley and the rural pastels of catalogue furnishings. In their drawing room they recreate a meadow. We think we love the country but most of us actually don't want to live there. We'd rather create what we think the country is in the town, where you can find a decent deli and something to do after nine o'clock at night.

Still lurking at the back of our minds is a shared cultural image of the reality of urban living. When Dickens invented Coketown, the archetypal Victorian city, in *Hard Times* he summed up what we think is the nightmarish vision of a metropolis. He wrote of the dense smog, brick that would be red if it were not for the infernal smoke which had blackened it, and rivers that flow purple with dye. Robert Southey, the Victorian Poet Laureate, in his essay 'Sir Thomas More', described the inhabitants of industrial cities 'like the dogs at Lisbon and Constantinople, unknowed, unbroken to any useful purpose, subsisting by chance or by prey, living in filth, mischief, wretchedness, a nuisance to the community where they live, and dying miserably at last'. Admittedly this may not altogether fit the memories of your last trip to Waitrose, but you can read rainforests of this kind of Victorian literature whose grip on our imagination and sense of the city is very strong. Lacerating condemnations of the immorality, sexual and political, of city life inspire these writers' adjectival skills to

Everest-like heights, either in the spirit of reform in Dickens's case or in order to sing the praises of the rural, the nostalgic. In the British mind there's Sodom and Gomorrah, the twin urban chambers of horror. And there's Little Beeding-on-the-Marsh. And we know where we want to live. In Little Beeding, where they have village greens and niceness and manners.

To a certain extent our reaction to this for several decades has been to flee the public spaces in cities in Britain. That has started to reverse as architects and planners and developers recognise the potential of the inner city once more. City living has begun to be fashionable again. What we used to call tower blocks, and hate, are now called tall buildlings, and worshipped. But many people just fled to the suburbs over the years. The cliché is 'an Englishman's home is his castle'. In fact, an Englishman's garden is his castle. We have deserted public space for the haven of our own fenced-off private spaces. We go 'into town' and then flee back to the haven of home, where we look over the fence. We even chat over the fence. One friend of mine has her herbal remedies dispensed over the fence. But the presence of the fence and the sanctity of our gardens represent the extent to which we have abandoned shared spaces for private ones. We don't take the responsibility for the space where we are 'polished' with one another. Our manners suffer because we fall out of the habit of consideration for each other. At the front of shops, shopkeepers sweep the litter and fag ends away from their own front door. They don't sweep it up: they sweep it out into the common space. People dump fridges, bicycles and all sorts on to the pavement. People quite openly throw litter and rubbish into the streets perhaps in the hope that roaming animals, dogs and goats possibly, will see it and shout, or bark and bleat 'buffet' as they gambol towards the mess to hoover it up.

What we seem not to have at the moment is what the sociologist Robert Putnam called in his book *Bowling Alone* 'generalised reciprocity'. I am trying to avoid saying that we used to have it but we've lost it. To some extent we did, but because we had a great deal less freedom. However, what certainly was bequeathed by the Second World War was a sense of unity of purpose. Bob Orrell, a D-Day veteran I interviewed about the sixtieth anniversary celebrations said simply about the war:

The whole of our lives revolved on this single act – there was nothing else in those days; we just had to beat the Germans. Life was easy really because you had no choices; you had just one fixed direction and you were wholeheartedly into it. I find it interesting these days because life then was easy. You didn't know what the bloody hell was going to happen or what was going to land where, but you had an unquestioning aim.

And that unquestioning aim bred a unity of purpose. It meant that individual desires could to a certain extent be subsumed within a collective good. Certainly there is now less sense of that as we are increasingly driven to pursue individual personal goals and wealth with, at best, a fragmented sense of national purpose. It is less conceivable in the world we currently live in that we should give up something for the greater good.

The Second World War gave us the collective success stories of the victory over fascism: the D-Day landings, Arnhem, Dunkirk, the POW camps, the Resistances in Europe. The list is a very long and proud parade of sacrifice. Later generations have simply never had an experience like that of such intensity for so long. We still stand in awe to some degree of what the few gave to the many. Everything around us these days is telling us to win for ourselves, yet we are tantalised by the prospect of being part of something bigger than just us. We are living in the contradiction between the single-minded pursuit of our own desires and a deep feeling, often identified as nostalgia, for a more collective and collaborative life. Manners in public require restraint, not a quality much praised in an era of emotional diarrhoea. We certainly don't need to button up again, shove our feelings, our desires, our sexuality into the back of the closet. But we might recognise that the myopic pursuit of our own desires is another factor eroding even further any attempt to breed manners in public places.

So what need *not* concern you when you're in the street or the city?

There are only two things:

- Whether to walk on the outside of a woman on the pavement – an etiquette book standard, this. I am as keen as the next Elizabethan to put my cloak over a puddle, as avid as the next Victorian, to protect my lady companion from the splash of Sherlock Holmes's carriage as he speeds on his way to solve the Reigate Puzzle. But while you might want to protect a child or an older person from the risk of being pushed off the pavement into the road, it strikes me that in this century women are pretty well able to cope without the assistance of men on the pavement. The only exception to this may be at night. If you are a man walking up behind a woman on her own, make sure you pass her and in so doing give her a wide berth so she knows you're no threat.

- Women smoking in the street. Oh tish, tosh, how unladylike. It's not women, or smoking, or doing it in the street – or the combination – that is the problem. The final destination of the butt is the issue, whether it's discarded by a boy or a girl.

Everything else on the street and in cities matters. Because that's where we meet strangers most. Oh dear what a responsibility, but here goes with an imperfect, or at least incomplete, list.

A

ATM/CASH MACHINES

Stand back, don't behave as if you're trying to peek. It intimidates people. Especially if their card gets eaten by the machine because they haven't got any money left. In the days when Lloyds, I think it was, had a glass window that slid up when you put your card in, I put a fish supper down on the ledge that the glass revealed while I punched in my PIN. It was late on a Friday night and I didn't have as much of my capability for multi-skilling left as I'd like to have had. After three botched attempts at the number, the machine ate my card. Before I could think, the window came down. It trapped my fish and chips, which now started to steam up the glass. The person behind me had been standing politely far enough back that she hadn't seen what had happened. So when I rather pathetically tried to explain and asked her if she'd put her card in to release my supper, she turned on her heels and ran. But, apart from when the person in front of you gets their takeaway trapped in the ATM, stand well back.

B

BICYCLING

Bicyclists think they are immune from the rules of the road. They charge up one-way streets the wrong way and gleefully ignore traffic lights. But although they kid themselves it's fine, it's actuallly very difficult for others to read what they are going to do. Let's face it, it's very convenient for them and very inconsiderate to everyone else. Cycling up a one-way street the wrong way, for instance, throws the pedestrian who expects traffic to be coming from one direction only. Likewise, it confuses drivers. And no amount of pleading that you're a vegetarian and morally superior to car owners by contributing to global warming less than them, even though the level of their veggie flatulence probably rivals the CO_2 emissions, absolves them from following the highway code. It's good manners because it makes other people's lives easier. And never bicycle on the pavement. You might as well wield a chain saw in a crowd. It's dangerous. You've got wheels: you belong on the road.

C

CHEWING GUM

A particularly choleric director once exploded at a well-known actress as she chewed gum all the way through rehearsals: 'For God's sake, stop chewing; you look like a cunt on a bicycle, darling.' It may not make you a better actor, but there are all sorts of reasons why chewing gum is a good idea, from masking bad breath to helping you stop smoking. But here's a fact. According to Keep Britain Tidy there are an estimated three hundred thousand pieces of discarded gum on Oxford Street in London. And councils spend £150 million a year cleaning gum off the streets. That's what it costs to educate about twenty thousand pupils a year. And if they were at school they wouldn't be out on the street chucking down gum. If it is them. And none of you are going home until someone owns up.

Put it in the wrapper. And throw it in a bin so that the rest of us don't get it stuck on our clothes, shoes or worst of all our bum if we sit in it.

D

DOGS

We love dogs. We hate poo.

It's that simple.

So scoop it.

DRIVING

Do we drive differently in the country than we do in the city? Yes. In the country the worst that can probably happen is that you get stuck behind a tractor. Or some sheep. Your valve starts to blow and steam comes out of your ears. But what can you do? Well, enjoy the view, I say. Hooting at sheep or tractor drivers is pointless. They both have very little sense of urgency. And they certainly have no desire to speed anything up just for us. Even if sheep had any kind of conceptual grasp of that, why would they care? All they want is a haircut and a painless death. Farmers live their lives waiting for harvest, so they're hardly going to speed up to give you five minutes more of your life. So, apart from not burning up rural lanes, there's less you can do in the country to put other people at risk.

In the city, though, given the way we drive, it is astonishing that the human race has survived this far. We seem to have made a ground-breaking scientific discovery. We have managed to locate the very essence of selfishness. If we could bottle it and give it to nuns, charity would cease forthwith. We've found the selfish engine. We're living with 4×4 monomania. We behave with more short-sightedness when driving than at any other time in our lives.

Yet if only he realised. Manners could make white van man. Or blue Mercedes man or red Mini man. Or woman for that matter. Even parents taking their children to school so they can to learn to behave like model citizens demonstrate the exact opposite to their little dears in the car. Because everyone on the road refuses to cede to anyone else's wishes. Some years ago two men in two cars came bonnet to bonnet in a lane behind a friend's house in Brixton. It was only wide enough for one car. Neither of them would reverse. So one of them took the only sensible course of action: he hit the other with the wheel jack. And the guy almost died. Drivers are role models only for the homicidal or egomaniacs. Driving threatens to become the nemesis of manners in cities.

And the funny thing is that we all know that when we're not driving. But when we are, there is nothing to be said except:

- Don't go into the yellow crisscross.
- Don't park where you'll block the traffic.
- Let people in in front of you.
- Don't speed. Keep calm or you'll kill someone.

- Don't scream at other drivers or you'll eventually have a heart attack.
- Be patient.
- Don't barge into traffic and block two lanes.
- Don't cut people up.

As you read this I know you're all nodding furiously in agreement. 'Oh yes, he's so right. I do agree. It's the only way. Absolutely. Hear, hear. How sensible.' And we'll all behave like that until, like a vehicular Superman, we are all transformed into Mr Toad by the fabulous metal box we like to call our own personal space. With driving we're like goldfish. We all remember how to behave considerately on the road. Until the next time, when we come round the front of the bowl and we've forgotten again. Expletives are undeleted and genital abuse is hurled out of the window at anybody else on the road and especially, therefore, in our way. Until we get home and complain furiously about people's driving. 'What dreadful manners people have on the road.' Yes, darling.

DRUNKEN BEHAVIOUR

Somebody once made the wise point that if you can remember to drink a pint of water before you go to bed to prevent a hangover the next day, you weren't drunk enough to need it. You really do wonder why we drink so much when we know that in the morning our mouths will feel like Velcro and taste like the compost bucket. And that cats will sound as if they are wearing heavy boots. And it's not as if what happens when we take a little refreshment is a twentieth-century discovery. In Dionysiac legend there were ten stages through which drink took you: health, love and pleasure, sleep (at which stage, the poet points out, the wise then go home), then arrogance, yelling, prancing about, black eyes, the police, vomiting, insanity and hurling the furniture. So what's new?

Drink is so wonderful you do marvel at how we came so to abuse it. The taste, the smell, what it does for us, at first are just the epitome of conviviality. But the final effect is so completely the opposite, as it takes us through every stage of manners from shyness, to being charming and charmed, to provoking the worst and most regretted behaviour we ever inflict on our friends or people we'll never meet again until they are witnesses against us in court.

Drink invades public spaces in cities. Any policeman will tell you that pretty much all they do on Friday and Saturday nights is deal with the effects of drink and drugs. So what of manners and drink? Do we have to fall back on 'in moderation only' so that when we drink we will retain at least the minimum level of respect for ourselves and for others? Well, not necessarily; it's not always about the amount you drink. Some people are lovely drunks. They improve with time in the presence of alcohol just like the wine they are drinking. Their manners are impeccable, if their demeanour a little fuzzy. But then there are people whose Mr Hyde appears disarmingly soon after their Dr Jekyll has taken a sip. A couple of drams and they're abusing the entire world, whether they know them or not. Or, in fact, whether they know anything about them or not. Roaming the streets after barely a pint they develop Tourette's to the world. They are a menace. They are very bad-mannered. And they almost invariably hit people.

The streets are full of both types and are mixed with the largest group of drunks to whom the very sight of a pub seems to be more of a challenge than a pleasure. These are the ordinary British. We are not alcoholic but we seem to live in a culture that is unable to conceive of pleasure without booze. It's essentially a philosophical problem. The necessary and specific quality of the category of 'enjoyment' is that it must contain at least 4 per cent volume and the sugar must have turned to alcohol. In Britain it's to be a sissy not to have a 'real' drink. Go on. Have a proper one. Instead it should be bad manners to press someone to drink what they do not want. We have managed to build up a considerable taboo about drinking and driving. If we are to have better manners around drink we need to build up as strong a sense of restraint around drinking without vehicular accompaniment. Do we need adverts, perhaps, hinting that sexual prowess is less affected by cranberries than lager?

When drinking, the general rule must be that you exercise restraint or at least to the extent that you remain not just conscious, but conscious of the need to be considerate. The Iteso of East Africa have beer parties, which last anything between five hours and three days. They sit in concentric circles, drinking through long straws from communal pots of beer. There are all sorts of rules about how you hold the straw, who can talk when, and the fact that women aren't allowed to crawl under the straws. But even they appoint someone to watch out for drunken behaviour and send a person home if they get out of order. Which, after drinking for three days, would seem a bit of a racing certainty, I would have thought.

There are extremes of drinking and our tolerance of it. Self-respect cannot encompass vomiting. Great hordes of shouting drunks and drunkesses on the streets, invading everyone's territory, must be bad manners. But, on the other hand, a hen night that serenades you in a restaurant, entirely out of tune but by way of an apology for making so much noise, with 'Sorry Is The Hardest Word' is not too hard to forgive.

F

FOOTBALL MATCHES

More than any other sport, although others are catching up, football is bedevilled by professionalism. When nineteen-year-olds win the Lottery of being the 'next David Beckham', when Manchester United pay almost £30 million for Wayne Rooney, the investors want a return. Play on the field reflects this. The pressure to win for reasons other than the spirit of the game seems to have created a sport where fouling is endemic, where what you can get away with defines the standard of behaviour and where Gary Lineker was seen as exceptional for simply being a clean player. Manners have taken a bit of a tumble in this situation.

As much as football builds a sense of community among teams' fans, it of course produces warring among rival tribes. And while fans on the same side take a surprising amount of care of each other and display great loyalty to their home towns and cities, their hostility for the opposition knows few boundaries. Good manners should be the attempt to reduce hostility, to manage the reflection off the pitch of the ritualised conflict on it. Fans and the football industry have recognised this to an extent in relation to racism. It is simply not acceptable behaviour – if you like, it's bad manners – to display racism on or off the pitch. Clubs get penalised and players get disciplined.

But no one seems to be able to control a remaining rump of fans who persist in hurling abuse and more often furniture at anyone who looks like they might be a rival. As much as fans bonding together is admirable when it is good-natured, large groups of people seldom behave with much consideration for those cast aside in their wake, those whose front gardens are weed on, whose Saturdays are disrupted by drunken loutishness.

Manners in all sport probably flow ultimately from the field, the pitch, the court and even the chess board. Those of us who want better manners in sport may have little left to us than to appeal to its leaders. Where contempt for the referee's authority is a badge to be kissed, gaining the fans' approval and fuelling the ratings, the television companies who broadcast the games, and the FA who seem so inadequate to oversee the sport, need to feel under pressure to make the game 'beautiful' once again. There is a watershed on TV. Perhaps football and its violence should be shown after it, leaving some room for love and sex before nine.

G

GIVING UP YOUR SEAT

After please and thank you, this is the one of great signifiers of manners, because it's one of the most visible gestures of consideration for others. And when it happens people really notice. The fact that there are signs prompting us to give up our seats suggests that we need to be asked. We don't do it automatically. On tubes they tell us that a particular seat is reserved for people who are old, disabled or women who are pregnant. It's a statement of the obvious really. Test it by thinking of the opposite: 'Please sit tight in your seat and, in fact, if you could hide behind your newspaper and pretend you can't see the pregnant woman with calipers desperately holding on to her elderly mother for support, that would be even better.'

You don't really need to think about whom you should give your seat up to. Someone who needs it more than you would be the rule. And you don't really have to have qualified in the means testing section of the Department of Social Security to work that out, now do you?

GROOMING (in public)

Nancy Mitford used to say that the triple stigmata of non-U was a woman wearing trousers, combing your hair in public and anything plastic.

Why is sitting opposite a woman brushing her hair or making herself up on the train fine, while sitting near a man or woman cleaning and cutting their nails is not? When either of them is filing them discreetly we probably don't mind that much. If they're on the other side of the aisle in the bus or the train, they're far enough away. But if they're on your table, then they're too close unless you live with them. Well, what fine distinctions we have developed in squeamishness. Monkeys wouldn't stand for it. They nit-pick constantly. We only nit-pick about what grooming is permissible in public.

Most people still hold taboos about what behaviour should remain private. Curiously, in an age in which we see sex on screen a great deal, we still seem to be more squeamish about someone on a bus or train slurping a drink or chomping food and sounding like a horse eating an apple. It may be a gesture not just to give up your seat when you should but to give up grooming and eating when you're around others.

L

LITTER

Some of us will go to our graves like Butterfly McQueen, the actress who forever regretted playing the little servant girl Prissy in *Gone with the Wind*, who died having dedicated her life to the removal of litter from the world. Or at least from the streets of towns in the state of Georgia and in New York. And she managed to combine this part-time career of Wombling with an increasing dislike of organised religion. Her point was that while Christians were only concerned with the streets of Heaven she wanted to make the streets on earth beautiful first. And she had a point.

You can get to Heaven a lot quicker than you'd expect, though, if you challenge people who drop litter on the streets in Britain. They take it badly. At a roundabout once, when I was on my bike, I threw an empty fag packet back in through the window of the Volvo out of which it had just come. The driver tried to run me over.

And then there's tidy littering. That's when they take the rubbish and ever so carefully place it on an outside windowsill or put a can ever so neatly at the foot of a lamppost. Is their mother popping by later to tidy up behind them? No, if they think at all, they think 'we pay our taxes and they'll sweep the streets'. Well, at least by clearing up the council has the good manners to think about other people when it comes to litter. But shouldn't we just not throw it down in the first place?

Challenging people when they drop litter will be one of the most visible signs of the campaign for better manners because it is such an outward display of consideration to the community. So, you may have a few rough rides, but challenge away. Maybe just a disingenuous 'I think you may have dropped something' might be a start.

LIFTS

To let people out of a lift before you try and get in is as obvious as not using them in a fire. Although when I see that sign 'Do Not Use Lift In Event of Fire' I do wonder whether it is going against the principles of natural selection. Surely people who would do so are some considerable way down the food chain.

But the main thing about lifts is that they are confined spaces, he says with the blinding insight of Galbraith or Hobsbawm. So when you're in them, you're in hand-to-hand combat with others for space. In a crowded lift you will touch other people. Make as much room as you can. Touching is not a taboo if done without menace or ambiguity. If you are at an airport with a trolley of luggage, go to the back. Make room for as many people as possible. You wonder why I am saying all this? Isn't it obvious? Well apparently not.

There is one amusing clash of culture that is very apparent in lifts. Westerners tend to whisper in lifts. Africans continue to shout as loudly as they do in the street. Sub-Saharans are not being rude when they raise their voices and Europeans are not plotting. Now you know. No need to be offended.

M

MOBILE PHONES

There is a story told. It is a legend among commuters on the Brighton to London line. It carries the hopes and dreams of anyone who has ever spent a train journey, a trip on a bus, a meal in a restaurant, a quiet evening in the pub drowned out by one half of barked conversations on a mobile phone belonging to the bloody person sitting next door to you. It goes like this. There is a man. An annoying man. Perhaps a successful man. Dressed, if not to kill, at least to commit some minor misdemeanour against taste and fashion. But he thinks he's pretty cool. 'Roger. No can do. Sales are pretty keen. A/c Kevin I'm now i/c the deal . . . Yes . . . No . . . It's not about what you know . . . Never . . . Not me . . . Them . . . Accounts.' Blah blah blah. His ego pours down his Nokia into the ether.

When there's finally a break in his loud, obnoxious torrent, the man opposite, instinctively knowing he is about to assuage the fury of the rest of the carriage with what he will do, rather sweetly compliments the man at some length on his phone. 'Oh yes, mate. Yeah. Top of the range.' Stealing up on his quarry very subtly, he then wonders whether it was expensive. It was. So is it very costly to insure? In fact not, the carriage discovers. In fact Mobile Man has a very good comprehensive deal indeed with relatively low premiums. So Quiet Man picks up the phone. And throws it straight out of the window.

I can hear you cheering now. Will it ever happen? Will pigs have wings? Will we ever have a quiet space in public again free from single-sided conversations? There has been a loss of the sense of division between public and private spaces because mobiles are dissolving privacy. We are all being forced to share one half of other people's lives. And we just don't care if they're 'on the train'. We are too. But because they are shouting at their friend, colleague, wife, husband, boyfriend, girlfriend, child or dog, we wish we weren't. We are unable to read, think or even tell them to shut up. We are inflicted by inanity. The kind of domestic trivia that bores us rigid in our own lives, we are now having to experience a thousand times a day, second-hand and in the half-light of guesswork about the rest of the conversation. You can't even eavesdrop with any great satisfaction. The only time it is truly funny is when some, usually young, man is forced into a romantic confession in front of us all on a bus: 'Yes. Me too. You know I do. I can't . . . I can't say . . . I'm on the train . . . I do you too . . . You know I . . . OK . . . I love you.' Then we can cheer.

There are a million reasons why mobile phones are just fantastic. And because they are so great, why can't we learn to use them with style and tact?

We all know the rules:

- Don't shout into them when others can hear.
- Don't assume that other people want to know your whereabouts.
- Don't just immediately answer them when you're talking to someone. Try saying 'Excuse me' or 'Would you mind if I take this?' or perhaps 'Would it be all right if I treated you and the conversation we are having with a little respect and ask your permission to break from it for a moment while I check on whether or not my good friend has pulled through this crucial operation and will live?' Because that is one of the very few conceivable reasons why you should be that rude.
- Don't leave them on during lunch or dinner.
- Don't leave them on in theatres, cinemas or at funerals and weddings. At funerals it's just hilarious in a ghastly sort of way as the ring seems to symbolise a message from the dead person. But I once heard a woman pick hers up and answer truthfully, 'I am at the National Theatre . . . It's very good . . . Yes, great acting . . .' The audience turned on her silently like mime vigilantes. No

noise. Just that British stare. The actors even stopped. And she had the cheek to remain utterly unembarrassed. The look on her face just said, as if we were all making a big fuss over nothing, 'Calm down. It was just my mother.' It had obviously been her mother's fault for ringing.

The same, incidentally, goes for headphones on public transport. When they are set too loud they sound like a bee with constipation or a wasp playing loo paper on a comb with a big beat boutique backing track. If we wanted to hear only the bass line and reverb of a CD we'd buy crappy stereos for our homes.

O

OPENING DOORS

Do you remember the character Millie Tant in *Viz*? She created so many moments when we laughed at feminism when we needed to but probably shouldn't have done. One of her best was when a man opened a door for her. She barged through and then over her shoulder yelled, 'Rapist'.

Open doors for people who need them opening. This is one of the simple ways we can acknowledge the fleeting bonds between us in a hurried life. And if you are the openee, for goodness sake reciprocate and say thank you.

P

PEEING IN PUBLIC

One night at Farringdon Station I wanted badly to pee before catching a train. The loos in the station had, of course, been vandalised. And, by the way, why vandalise loos? Beating up a loo has all the hallmarks of cowardly behaviour, kicking a pan when it's down and suchlike. Anyway, they were vandalised. And then I remembered a little park round the corner. So I snuck there. I checked whether I might be seen and so offend anyone. There was no one about. I went right to the corner where I could pee in the flowerbed so it would sink in and not run away in a stream across the path for someone else to see or stand in. So far so pretty damn considerate. I thought I had worked out all the possible principles to guide 'the peeing outside' section of the book. But when I mentioned the whole procedure to a friend who's a bit of an eco-bunny, he said, 'Well, what about the effect on the water table?' Oh, for goodness sakes.

If you have to go, the principles must flow from consideration for others. So don't offend anyone who might be offended by todgers and bums. And don't just pee anywhere. Find somewhere it can sink in. And remember: it's all much more problematic for girls. But the same rules surely apply.

What is not on is:

- Weeing in someone else's front garden on the way back from the pub/football/theatre/boxing/or even visiting your sick mother in hospital.
- Weeing on the pavement – if you must do it on the street, do it in the gutter – shouting out that you are doing it and pointing at yourself, which I saw a man doing only last November.

Q

QUEUES

People often go to the front of a queue and say 'I am in a terrible hurry, I need to go first.' But they only know their own situation. I often wonder how they can make a priority from a list of one? We British get laughed at across the world for knowing how to queue. Second only to the fact that we eat pickled onions and pork scratchings in pubs for pleasure, it is one of the things that sets the British apart. We are inordinately proud of it. It's an exercise in restraint, which in the classic theory of manners is at the very centre of the whole business. But doesn't it just make sense? Do we want every attempt to buy a train ticket, get on the bus or acquire a Double Whopper at Victoria Station to be a Darwinian crapshoot? Like it is when they open a new till in the supermarket. Or how it always is in Belgium? For goodness sake, be British. Stand in a line and wait your turn.

S

SPITTING

In the particular American states where everyone is cousins and there are too many banjos and not enough teeth, spitting was long associated with tobacco. Oscar Wilde once sniped on a visit, 'America is one long expectoration.' Phlegming it up was quite commonplace even in the White House for much of the nineteenth century. But even Erasmus was moved to warn the young man in 1530 to 'turn away when spitting to avoid . . . spraying on someone else. If any disgusting matter is spat onto the ground it should . . . be ground underfoot lest it nauseate someone.'

There are moments when you just have to spit out a horrible taste. For fear of libel I will not mention the restaurants. And if there's poison, spitting may save your life. Although maybe into a tissue rather than on the floor would be good. Apart from emergencies, though, spitting has been disapproved of for centuries in Europe. In China, however, it is still quite the done thing to hawk away, even for animals. In the Zhengzhou Zoo in Henan province in central China, they had a thirteen-year-old chimpanzee called Feili who, having turned to smoking, started to beg cigarettes from visitors. When they refused he spat on them. In the human realm, a sign of great contempt, there was also an outbreak of spitting on Christian priests in Jerusalem by yeshiva students recently.

But the savage non-verbal expression of abomination and scorn apart, it's just not very healthy. Ever since the German biologist Robert Koch discovered the tuberculosis bacillus in 1882 and it was recognised that it could survive in saliva, spitting has by and large been regarded as not quite right in polite society. And a jolly good thing too. At the very least it's a health hazard. Even the French Hygiene Council issued an ordinance against it in 1886, though the Paris authorities still have to put signs in the Métro that read '*Défense de cracher*'. If they have signs, people must still be doing it. And we all say *Arrêtez-vous* this minute. Urgh.

TRAINS, TUBES, BUSES

One last word, on public transport. It is a characteristic of Britain that it's always worth running for the train. A friend of mine from Cape Town recently managed to hold one up for fifteen seconds in Switzerland. She is proud to have managed to bring a little African time to the land of the cuckoo clock. In Britain, though, life is a gamble. At four minutes past, it's still worth racing for the seven minutes to. So on that basis it must be good manners and considerate behaviour to hold up the train, tube or bus by holding the door to let people on. They're going to be late anyway. This is Britain.

—∽∿∽—

4

TABLE MANNERS

Table manners are one of the most fraught areas of social behaviour. People are terrified of them. Or at least of getting them wrong. Fear of the existence of some unseen, and more disturbingly unknown, rule book hangs like a sword of Damocles over us. Since I told anyone that I was writing this book, I can't go to dinner without people bombarding me with anxieties about whether the table is laid properly. Is the wine the right one to go with the food? Have they seated the guests correctly? Should the cheese follow the dessert. Oh my God, is it called dessert or pudding? Which way should the port be passed? It goes on and on.

Normally confident and secure individuals, high achievers at home and at work, people who wore shoulder pads in the eighties, the world's most expensive trainers in the nineties and in the noughties have well-adjusted children at university and portfolio careers, start to waver under the tyranny of the soup spoon. They can cut their suppliers at work down to a better price in three pithy sentences, run their local charity and analyse Third World debt and its relationship to colonialism. But they are gripped by insecurity about whether it really is okay to drink red wine with fish.

But in all honesty there's no need to worry. The big thing with table manners, for either guest or host, is to realise that the rules laid down by the Wagnerian *über*-dwarfs of etiquette that purport to contain the party rules of entertaining were invented by the Supper Stasi not to make eating together more enjoyable but essentially to make you feel excluded when you didn't know them. And therefore make them feel superior because they did. These rules just don't, by and large, help you in the great convivial exercise of eating with people round your table; rather, they turn what should be the most companionable and relaxed experience into a snobbery assault course that only the hardest crack commandos can complete. So you can calm down. Eating together is about getting on with each other. I know it sounds a bit simple, but it is true. There really is only one basic rule at meals and it explains all you need to know. You can express the fundamental purpose of sharing food together if you think about the knife.

In modern Western cultures there are two basic ways that people hold their knife at the table. The first is to clasp the shaft between the thumb and the second finger, the third and fourth fingers are tucked round the handle to grip it, and the index finger is on the top of the blade pushing down on the food. At this point there should be a Fig. 1, I know, but you're an intelligent reader.

The second way is to hold the knife like a pen.

The latter was regarded by people like my mother as simply beyond the pale. Holding your knife like that indicated that you were, through no fault of your own probably, a stranger to natural fabrics, regrettably had used the word 'cruet' more than once in your life and more than likely had a 'settee' in your 'front room' (or worse 'lounge'). People who hold their knife like that call it neither pudding nor dessert but, oh no, oh dear, they call it 'the sweet'. Simply ghastly. And frankly 'common'. But in the history of eating together and in the fundamental reasons why we do it and derive pleasure from it, there is no distinction to be drawn between these two. Except, of course, a class one. The only important thing with a knife is that you don't hold it like a violent weapon, clenched in your fist, raised and ready to plunge into the heart of your guest rather than into the food. That is the only wrong way to hold it, because most table manners have grown from the need to reduce the possibility of hostility or violence between those of us eating together. Table manners flow from one simple basic principle. Don't confuse the guests with either the food or the enemy. Don't eat them and don't kill them.

As hosts and guests we agree to negotiate with each other. At dinner at someone else's house, on someone else's territory, we are more careful about what we talk about or at least how far we push it. A particularly attractive, clever and well-known economist told me once that she frequently gets the 'how-come-a-pretty-girl-like-you-knows-so-much-about-the-relationship-of-the-dollar-to-the-yen' approach from some smug, older male baboon at dinner. But when I asked her how she responded to people like that, she said it depended how good a friend the host was. In the end, offensive as Mr Smug was being, the easy atmosphere of the dinner and her friendship with the host mattered much more to her than the behaviour of the antidiluvian in pinstripes (I'm guessing at the pinstripes, and adding one of those coloured shirts which have a plain white collar and cuffs). Her response is classically good manners because it honours the rule that when we eat together we aim for ease not violence. Even when we choose to argue, manners guide us to do it with care so that it doesn't spiral out of control and risk a fight. Manners can't be about what you think. But they can be about what you do. The reason to eat together is beyond food. It's to see if we can find ways of communicating, of managing our difference. We don't do it to agree a joint manifesto in every detail of a future together. We do it to find common ground with each other. And how much you find dictates whether, if you're the host, you ask them again, if you're a guest, whether you accept, and for both whether you seek each other out. This is true whether it's you and I or world leaders eating together in the hope that peace may break out. You may remember from your schooldays the Field of Cloth of Gold in 1520. It's one of only three dates that I can remember. It was a meeting between Henry VIII and Francis I of France near Calais. They ate for days. Big tents, big food, all in the cause of the English mediating in the Habsburg-Valois wars with Holy Roman Emperor Charles V.

Meals together are profound in their own way because eating together, sharing food, is the most basic social bonding mechanism that humans practise. Animals do not share food except with their young or the family pack. No giraffe has ever had a dinner party. No baboon has asked the neighbours in for a fondue. No lion has entertained its boss with beef and wine it couldn't afford. But food is easily divided and often shared between humans and eaten together to create harmony. And, just to reiterate, it works a lot less well as a bonding mechanism if you try and kill or eat your fellow diners.

The only people who break this rule with studied regularity are cannibals. And even they have table manners. There are two types of cannibals: those that eat their own, especially relatives, and those that only eat enemies. Endo and exo, they're called. The latter, while not exactly a worldwide rage any longer, are more common than the former. Which is a relief to anyone who has been to any kind of family reunion recently.

Nonethless, and rather curiously, cannibals have very clear rules about eating people. While cannibalism seems needlessly vicious and out of control, it is thought by those who practise it to serve a purpose, often to strengthen those who eat. Margaret Visser quotes a number of scary descriptions of cannibalistic rites in her book *The Rituals of Dinner*. In the Aztec gladiatorial sacrifices – and the Aztecs were peculiarly keen on such things and worryingly skilled at them – the unfortunate captive was tied by the waist to a sacrificial stone, given a sword but then attacked by the warriors from the capturing tribe. The stone in this case was a kind of fatal golf handicap. Then just before the victim died, his blood was drained into a green bowl with a feathered rim, he was skinned and his flesh was cut up and eaten. This was all highly ritualised. There were strict rules. It was often the case, for instance, that the man who ultimately did the killing didn't eat the victim. The Aztecs did this kind of thing so often that it is just as well that they were exo rather than endo. If they had been half as successful at eating their relatives as they were at eating the enemy, there would have been even fewer of them left than there are now.

What is important about all this, though, is that even when cannibals were eating other people they practised some kind of restraint. In other words they had manners. Albeit not so much table manners as sacrificial stone manners. What seems like a mad grab for inhumanity, a kind of culinary anarchism taken to the furthest point, did in fact have boundaries. It was in some way institutionalised in the societies which practised it. And while it was terrifically violent there were rules, discovered by anthropologists like Lévi-Strauss who argued that in the cannibal world it was prestigious to be roasted but a bit common just to be boiled. It's the same for us with potatoes, I guess. Boiled is dull, sautéed is still thought positively chichi. And there were, of course, rules about whom you should eat and whom you shouldn't. This is particularly the case with endos. But then all families do tend to be a bit picky about each other.

One place to start to decode table manners and set yourself at ease, once you've decided that your dinner party won't end up in a ritual sacrifice, is with the realisation that the words 'host' and 'guest' have the same root. They both come from the Indo-European word *ghostis* which means 'stranger'. It used to annoy me, in the way that people who wear Birkenstocks and sensible clothing always have done, that over-enthusiasts from the Youth Hostelling movement, the Scouts and other associated fun fascists, would beam at you 'a stranger is just a friend you haven't made yet'. But dammit, you know, they're right. It's no coincidence that hostility and hospitality have the same root. In Latin *hostis* means stranger, which leads to the English 'hostile'. In French the word *hôte* means 'guest' and 'host'. And in all cultures both are essentially strangers who can become friends over a meal. We all participate in this process when we eat together. Eating together becomes a way of increasing our knowledge of each other, our warmth to each other and of dissolving any residual hostility, actual or, if you want to be very poncy about it, existential, between each other. Table manners are the rules that help that to happen.

So the way you hold your knife is to do with not showing violence. Saying grace is just the chosen way of religious people to create the much more important sense that we are conscious of eating together as a group not just as a bunch of unassociated individuals. Not eating with your mouth open is about not showing your teeth which are potential weapons. Most of us were told not to eat with our elbows on the table. Well to us, and eaters in fairly modern times, that indicates that we are exercising a degree of restraint. We are sitting up, which is slightly unnatural. And that physical effort indicates politeness. The Greeks, on the other hand, reclined when they ate and so would Jesus have done. So they had to eat with their elbows on the table otherwise they'd fall into the soup. As Margaret Visser points out, the Greek text of the Bible says that John was 'on his master's breast'. If you try and paint him that way sitting in a chair, as they did in the sixteenth century, he has to look up like a puppy leaning on Jesus's shoulder. The only reason to point this out is just to show that the rule about no elbows on the table didn't come down from the mountain on tablets of stone. It developed with chairs and it demonstrates restraint, a theme of all manners.

Over the passage of time meals have become bewilderingly overladen with rules. In Emily Post's latest edition there are ninety-six different foods, each of which has its different eating etiquette. It's come a long way from the simple hunter-gatherer society. How easy it must have been then. Kill the food. Eat the food. Burp. Now we have moved a long way into another phase of civilisation – although, in my view, not up or down the road of progress, just along it. Now someone else kills the food or grows it. And you're not supposed to burp – at least not in Britain. Unless you're in Britain with Turks or Middle Easterners. Or as Margaret Visser, whose comprehensive authority on these matters is over-awing, points out, if you go to China, Japan or various African countries where it's generally fine, in fact often a sign of appreciation of the food, to let out a great big, pleasurable belch at the end. The Pedi of South Africa have even got a particular onomatopoeic name for the appreciative post-dinner eruption: *pôtla*.

For half the time we eat now someone else even cooks our food. We used to forage; now we make reservations. Or stay in with takeaways or TV dinners. And somewhere along that line from the cave to the Conran canteen, the etiquette elves decided to work night after night over years and years to try and think up rules that would make eating food the most uncomfortable and difficult process known to the world. Instead of the basic principles of good manners, respect and ease, being applied to eating, the supposedly very smart people set up a series of tripwires for the uninitiated between the front door and the cheese course to make sure that, if the rest of us weren't kept out, we were at least identified as intruders.

They have invented rules about when you arrive, when you leave. What wine to bring, what wine to drink with what kind of food. How to hold the wine glass, whether to use coasters, what to do with your pre-dinner drink when you go to the table, which way to pass the port. How to lay the table. Whether knives and forks should face in, out, up or down. Whether to use table mats or a tablecloth. Where to put the flowers. Whether to use candles. Whether to compliment the food or not. Whether to take seconds. Whether when you're drinking tea the milk goes in first or last. Whether your little pinkie finger should stick out when you're drinking tea. Where to seat the most important woman. How to seat twelve people in order of rank at a widow's house. (Honestly. Emily Post spent enough time thinking about this to reach the conclusion that it was impossible.) Whether you can mop up your gravy, sup it from your plate or use a spoon. Whether you can pick up the food with your fingers, throw bread in your soup, help yourself or be served. Whether to put napkins on the side plate, by the side plate, above the side plate, in the garden, on the back seat of the car. I know. I am just getting bored now and making it up. But having read so many etiquette books, after a while the mind begins to boggle that the middle and upper classes apparently had that much time to think up such idiotic trivialities. The answers to most of these questions are different customs in different cultures and classes. But now we've established some basic principles of eating together, here's another incomplete, imperfect list of things that matter and things that don't.

THINGS THAT JUST DON'T MATTER IN THE GREAT SCHEME OF IT ALL

These are things that you can certainly look up in etiquette books or trace the history of, if you have a burning interest in minutiae. One of my favourite titles on this kind of subject is *European Spoons Before 1700*, by J. Emery. Don't all rush now. And then there's *Pocket Knives at Table? Whatever Next* by S. Moore. I can feel the stampede.

But, interesting as all this may be, it is not central to the idea of manners at the table. The biggest effect of these kind of rules is to make people just feel very nervous. And that rather defeats the point of manners. So what really need *not* concern you around your table or when you go out to someone else's house are the following:

- How to lay the table.
- The entire subject of flowers on the table.
- Napkins and where to shove – sorry – put them.
- Candles.
- Which kind of glasses to use. (If you're a wine drinker, there is some useful and enjoyable advice to be gleaned from a whole variety of wine books on which glasses best serve the taste of the wine, and what temperatures brings out the best flavours, and the kind of different grapes and vintages and types of wine that work wonderfully with different foods. And if you're a spirit drinker the Scotch Malt Whisky Society recommends how much and what kind of water best brings out the wonderful whiff and warmth of a whisky, its taste and its smell. But none of that has anything to do with the idea of manners.)
- Whether you serve the food or people help themselves (the only point here is if a guest has one arm, no hands, legs they can't use, are blind, old or in some way unable to help themselves at the table or from anywhere else. Rule: ask them

quietly if they want help. Don't single them out, but do try and move your lips when you talk to them. Don't do she's-had-a-hysterectomy-speak as if you're gossiping over the garden fence like Les Dawson.)

- Whether cheese or pudding is the last course. (the French like to end sweet, the Brits savoury. I cop out and put both on the table at the same time, but that's not manners or etiquette, it's just a preference. Make yours.

THINGS THAT ARE WORTH THINKING ABOUT

There are ten different features of eating together that are definitely worth thinking about:

- Invitations.
- Whom to invite.
- Food.
- Arriving.
- When to arrive, what to bring to dinner and, if you're the host, what to do with it.
- Starting to eat.
- Where people sit.
- Conversation.

- Farting, belching, elbows on the table and other bugbears.
- Children at the table.

Invitations

The biggest problem with invitations is how to turn them down. Accepting is dead easy. 'Do you want to come to dinner at mine on Thursday?' 'Yes.' 'Eight-ish?' 'Great.'

It's turning them down that's so difficult. So if you ring people to invite them, the general principle would be to try and avoid putting them in a difficult position from the off. Make it easy for them to say no, if they want to. They may not want to come. It's almost inconceivable, I know. But they might not. For whatever reason. So when you ring try not to make it an open question like 'What are you doing Thursday?' Now they're trapped. So give people a get-out. It's the polite thing to do because it reduces potential social conflict. Giving them social wiggle room oils the wheels. When people do it to me, I always say a provisional 'yes' while claiming a possible, but as yet unconfirmed, work commitment. And then a couple of days later I phone back and say I'm sorry but no. Or more probably I act the real coward and write or e-mail, and say I'm sorry but I won't be able to come.

There is one person whom I really do not like who has been trying to invite me for dinner for quite a while now. He reminds me of a particularly predatory lizard. His dinner invitations are a reptilian tongue flicking out to catch a fly. I do not want to play in his cage in the zoo. So I'm still avoiding him. And with good reason. It's better to avoid going and avoid telling him why, than to go to dinner and distort the purpose of a meal together by not enjoying him, and probably his friends, and straining all night to create a bond that I don't want in the first place. The only basis on which I would go was if it was important to someone else. If your partner, your wife or husband or child or close work colleague for reasons best known to themselves likes someone and wants you to go. Then go. Maybe only once. But go. And you'll be going not because you like someone, but because you like, or in the case of your partner, love them.

There are many invitations that you feel obliged to accept for reasons that range from naked ambition to a genuine generosity in relieving someone's loneliness. Sup with the Devil if indeed you'll get promotion, but remember Faust. Hosts and guests are indebted to each other. And when you accept an invitation out of sympathy, kindness or obligation to someone else you need to learn gently to draw boundaries with your more-enthusiastic-than-you host. Otherwise it'll become like Japanese bowing. They invite you, you feel obligated to invite them back. They return what in the case of someone you really liked would be called the favour and so it goes on. It tests all the skills of good manners to extricate yourself without offending them and injuring the social bond. Just in case you're ever in Nepal you should know that sherpas have a disarming way of dealing with all this, as do the Javanese. Visser describes how the former just make it almost impossible for you to refuse. If you do, you risk causing tremendous offence to the host. One of their tactics is to send the invitation as a message delivered by a small child who invites you to the feast but can't actually tell you when it is. So you can't claim a prior engagement. You may well be keeping your diary free for the next ascent of Everest or waiting to buy tickets for a Tibetan Buddhist religious concert of a *mani-rimdu* dance-drama, but you can't use that as basis for refusal. The Javanese also use little children to invite friends, neighbours and family to what they call a *slametan*. In this case guests are required to come. In fact, the host only sends out the invitation after the food has already been laid out. You get barely a maximum of ten minutes' notice and have to drop everything and high-tail it to the party.

By and large it would be good to avoid either of

these techniques. Equally, don't invite people too far in advance. There's no wiggle room then, as which of us can really say what we will be doing in a month's time? Although some people are geniuses with excuses. Peter Cook was famously asked by David Frost to dinner a few weeks in advance in order to meet the Duke and Duchess of York (Andy and Fergie in happier, chubbier and more married days). Making some play of leaving the phone, ostensibly to look at his diary, he returned and said to Frost, 'I can't come. It seems I am watching television that night.' Not all of us have that kind of comic pluck.

The etiquette books are generally very clear about invitations. Emily Post, for instance, says that they must contain five basic elements. Paraphrased, they remind me of what they tell you on basic journalism courses. The first sentence of any article is always supposed to begin with Who? What? When? Where? and, optionally for the more metaphysical, Why?

'Noddy and Big Ears [who] demanded compensation [what] today [when] at a meeting of the Toy Town Council [where] for the injuries suffered to their dignity by being given a car with an unfeasibly pathetic horn and eponymous ears that singled out the gnomic one as Dumbo's cousin [why].' So, with an invitation make it easy for people to accept and to know what they're going to, when, where and at whose behest. And if you're going to send an invitaton by e-mail, or just confirm the details, make sure that you know they are the kind of person who checks their e-mails regularly.

Post's advice is thus a lot more helpful than *Debrett's*, who still think there are people, apart from the Queen and those curious charities that always seem to have an Austro-Hungarian princess called The Princess Taxi zum Clo und Rheinenstagenpfluffer über Menz or whatever as their patron, who give dinner parties so formal they need engraved invitations sent out at least a month in advance. *Debrett's* also suggests that if you don't do that, any verbal invitation should be followed up with a *pour mémoire* card. I know that's French, but it doesn't make it any more helpful.

One habit that infuriates hosts when they ask some-one to dinner is when the potential guest says, 'Who else is coming?' before they accept. To which I always reply, 'Well, now, not you!' I don't mean it, but I catch myself resenting the fact that for them apparently it's not enough just to be asked and that they don't trust me to invite people whom they will like, find interesting, know very well already or who might do them some good careerwise, if they are the kind of person who devotes most of their energy to clawing their way up the greasy pole of ambition. But, of course, asking who's going to be there does at least confirm once again that it's the people not the food that matters.

Finally, a splendid example of the last point was my godfather's wife Rosemary, long dead now, who was the most appalling cook. The car journeys back home from Sunday lunch at their house were the only times when, outside of an aeroplane, sick bags were compulsory in our family. The French are cruel to pets but wonderful with vegetables. Rosemary (not her real name, for the sake of her children whose ability to survive so many of her meals far outshines that of any guest of the Borgias) could maim vegetables and turn the most benign of meats into the deadliest weapon of poison. However, she gave the most brilliant parties. Full of sparkling people at their ease where the wit flowed as smoothly as the jellies that had never set or the egg mousse that you ladled like soup into your mouth for the first course. A brilliant hostess. And a lesson to us all, even though a Wimbledon Poisoner among cooks.

Invitations to meals that will nurture the bonds between us need to be clear, easy to accept and, although it feels counterintuitive, easy to turn down. People will continue to invite you to formal dinners with 'stiffies' but for a private do those kind of hard-card invitations are stentorian and very Victorian.

Invitations should just be warm and, if rather obvious to say so, inviting.

Whom to invite

There are some very jolly examples of casting dinners with curious guests through the ages. Heliogabalus is my favourite in this regard. He was Roman Emperor from the age of fourteen to eighteen (218–222) and he particularly liked inviting people on the basis of the oddness of their appearance: eight bald men, eight men with one eye, eight fat men and so on. And he had gay orgies which scandalised Rome. Now, whether they were with the one-eyed, bald or fat men doesn't seem to be recorded, but if you think what else went down until the Empire finally fell sometime in the fifth century, if they were a bit strong for the Romans they must have been pretty racy. Antonin Artaud wrote a play about him called *The Crowned Anarchist* and ever since I found out about him he's risen quite close to the top of my fictional dinner party guest list.

Casting a dinner party is a very enjoyable lark. It's a form of alchemy. Although most of us live lives where we don't have time to give it that much thought. And you never quite know what people will or won't have in common. I once interviewed together Dennis

Healey and Andrew Sachs, the actor who played Manuel in *Fawlty Towers*. Nothing in common there, you think, except a discussion on the role of Spanish waiters in the failing British economy under Labour in the 1970s. Until Andrew Sachs told the story of his father's internment as a Jew by the Nazis and his family's terrified flight from Berlin at the same time as the young, and then Communist, later Chancellor of the Exchequer, Dennis was on a comradely cycling trip with other young anti-fascists hoping to see for themselves the rising Nazi menace. Surprising commonalities flourish in fertile conversational ground, especially if you accept your responsibility as host and guests play their part as well.

Problems mainly arise, not when people don't know each other, but when you forget that they simply hate one another. At the most extreme end of this kind of unfortunate guest list are the obvious ones. I sincerely hope that the Grand Wizard of the Ku Klux Klan is not a friend of yours. But clearly don't invite him at the same time as your favourite Jewish intellectual. Leave the local BNP candidate for another time if you've asked the Head of the Commission for Racial Equality. You get the point. Much more difficult to deal with, though, are friends and family who don't like each other. You may be trying to help and a meal together may be your best chance of achieving a reconciliation, but you'll have to work overtime as host. The Gogo of Tanzania resolve quarrels by slaughtering a goat and removing its liver. At which point each side bites on the liver and the priest then cuts it in two and that way everyone is said to have kissed and made up. Although liver that raw is a little too pink for me, even for the sake of peace and reconciliation. Eating together may work to calm a dispute but it'll test all your skill, because when you're the host it's your responsibility to make sure that the party doesn't end up in a brawl, either intellectual or physical, nor in a flouncing out. Manners for the host is about managing the conflict. You can't just cook and lie back. Dinner is your Field of Cloth of Gold.

Food

People are getting a bit fussy these days. It used to be enough to throw an ox on the fire, ask round friends and people you wanted to make a treaty with and you had a party. Now what we win on the swings of diversity and personal choice we lose on the round-abouts of cultural and religious food preferences, vegetarianism and anaphylactic shock. Cooking for people becomes a potentially treacherous journey around an array of cultural and dietary requirements and silly fads. You do wonder what all those nut-intolerant people did before. When they wolfed down a Walnut Whip and died, did we just put it down to stress, heart failure or an unknown tropical disease? Maybe Susan Sontag was right: name a disease and then everyone gets it. Tell the world about nut allergies and suddenly there are warning signs everywhere. However we dealt with it before, it seems these days you simply aren't terribly interesting if you don't have a dietary complication.

I once gave a small supper for a Russian political campaigner visiting the UK so that he could meet some British counterparts. I didn't know most of them. So I sent out an e-mail asking if anyone had any kind of dietary prohibitions. Well, there were two anaphylactics, a couple of vegetarians, a pair of practising Jews, someone who had a mild, slightly allergic aversion to fungi and a woman who'd 'prefer not to eat anything killed without care'. Oh please. There was also a sugar-averse bisexual, three gluten intolerants and one woman I discovered, once the dinner was in full swing, was simply intolerant.

So I gave them a beef sirloin – salvaged from a bullfight – with shellfish, wrapped in a flour based mushroom sauce sprinkled with nuts and drizzled with a sweet balsamic dressing. I wish I had. But I accommodated all their needs, gave them pasta (gluten and non-gluten, of course) and hoped for the best. They are all still alive, as far as I know.

There's a very simple thought here, though. If you want to know whether your guests are going to die or come out in hives if you give them certain kinds of food, then ask. And if you are likely to die or come out in hives, then tell your host. There is a value to honesty if it's going to avert a trip to the mortuary or hospital. And don't be nervous about asking about people's dietary habits and behaviour at the table if the differences flow from a religious or ethnic root. There seems to be a cultural cringe at the moment, as if you have to tread on eggshells around difference (and treading on eggshells probably has immense and powerful significance in certain Papua New Guinean subcultures). But has our curiosity failed us? There is no need to worry about not knowing when you encounter a culture foreign to your own. Rather, it is good manners to ask. Discovery about difference means you can enjoy it. Not knowing means you have to live in a Helen Keller world of touch and guess. Manners are essentially inclusive. If they are there to promote ease between us, then cultural difference round a table has to be managed easily, directly and with enthusiasm.

Arriving

Letting people cross our threshold is terribly significant to us. We keep lots of people who ring our bell on the doorstep. My mother, who lived in a little village in the West Country, told a story against herself in the month before she died. A man called at her house, banged the knocker and when she opened the door, said by way of introduction: 'You don't know me, but . . .' Before he had time to go on, she smiled and said sweetly, 'Well, I suggest we keep it that way.' And closed the door.

Then she rang me and said 'I've done a terrible thing', before proceeding, with great relish, to tell me the story. I suspect she then rang her friends and told them too. She was indecently proud of her own wit. And, beside the fact that she didn't ask him in, was the way she did it good or bad manners? Well, it was a little rude on the face of it. But she was an old lady. She didn't know him and that makes people a potential threat when you're eighty-seven. Not necessarily a violent threat, but a threat to your pensioner's wallet whether you're convinced into a time share in Majorca, a new kitchen bucket or a not entirely healthy subscription to The Chocolate Club. What's interesting in the question 'good or bad manners?' is that because she was old and it was funny we laugh and we love her for doing it. Which means that we excuse it. Good or bad, you can argue it both ways. It was a witty way for her to defuse a potential threat or a not terribly polite way to deal with a stranger. Either way, she didn't ask him in.

And 'do come in' is a considerable gesture of welcome. In anthropological terms you are asking strangers, who are potentially dangerous, into where you are most vulnerable – your home. And in different cultures there are all sorts of ways in which we show that we are disarming ourselves. In Japan and the Middle East you take off your shoes. In Europe in the days when men carried sticks and wore hats, they left them in the hall. In fact, they handed them to the person who opened the door. In houses in certain townships in South Africa you are supposed to go right in and just take a seat, not to wait to be asked. This supposedly demonstrates trust. But hallways, certainly in Europe, America and Australia, are full of kissing and embracing.

The rituals of welcome are the way we cautiously introduce people into our house. But, of course, when people know each other really well – friends, family or neighbours who have keys to our house, for instance – all this goes by the board. They just let themselves in and head straight for the fridge. And we don't mind at all. If a stranger did it, though, we'd feel a little violated. A good, or, rather bad, example of this happened in my house at a birthday party I had. At about 2 a.m. the champagne that we'd been drinking most of the evening finally ran out. All that was left were a few particularly special bottles that had been brought as presents: a couple of magnums of Bolly and Tatty. You know the kind of thing. Actually, it was four bottles of Lanson. Anyway, they were tucked away in a cupboard still warm and waiting for a special occasion. And then I heard one of the corks pop. A woman, whom I didn't know and who had come with an acquaintance, had just helped herself. Good manners were in the balance. What to do? She had really offended my hospitality. On the other hand, if I wasn't to make her feel bad about it, I could play the 'perfect host' and smile and ignore it. She hadn't been invited, but she had come with someone who had. But he hadn't asked if he could bring her. She wasn't his partner, or even a good prospect. But then again I didn't know him that well. However, I would put him in an awkward position if I singled her out. But, then, did I mind if we never progressed beyond acquaintance? You can go on like this forever, trying to determine the greater loyalty and responsibility between guest and host. And to some extent it best illustrates the difference of how you behave to good friends and how much more cautious we should all be with strangers. She should have asked if she could open the bottle. I could then say yes or no, and have done it gently: 'I'd rather you didn't, if that's okay. I want to keep them and it's a waste to drink them warm. Would you like some wine instead?' You see, that would have worked. Rather well, in fact. Difficult, hostile situation avoided. But she hadn't asked. It was already a bit difficult.

What did I do? I decided not to ignore it. I did feel that my hospitality had been invaded and taken for granted by what she did. It upset a balance. Looking back, I realise it was the fact that she was a stranger and was so obviously not in the least concerned about being in someone else's house. So – and I am slightly blushing at this point, but, like my mother, still going to tell you the story – I asked her if she knew a good taxi number. 'Yes,' she replied. Then casually I said, 'Oh, have you got a mobile?' She had, she said holding out one of those little geisha girl-size mini mobiles. 'Well, I suggest you call for a cab then.' And I gently removed the glass from her hand. I don't feel that proud of what I did. Did we both behave with bad manners? I expect so. They left the house and the following day they left a bottle of champagne on the doorstep. And that was nice of them. The negotiation between guests and host is a very delicate one. So when you are in someone else's house, go carefully. As you cross the threshold take care. Take care, you tread on my beams. When you are in someone else's house you have to respect their space.

When to arrive, what to bring and, if you're the host, what to do with it

Don't arrive early. There is a delicate power share going on at meals and putting the host at a disadvantage is bit of an opening move in a subtle game of chess. This disrupts the basic balance between guest and host. On the other hand, if you're a good friend turn up early and help. Between friends, like so much of manners it's not an issue, but exactly when you are expected to show up at dinner if you're not a close mate is highly culturally specific and tends to relate to the temperature at which the food is expected to be eaten. In Western Europe food is by and large served and eaten hot. So guests pitch up no more than twenty minutes after the time of the invitation. In Japan apparently no one expects you much before an hour after you were invited and in Greece, where they don't eat food hot but warm, half an hour after the invitation is a bit early.

Whatever time you arrive, though, bring something with you. Unless you have come straight from hospital where your partner has just given birth, or from your mother's funeral, or from a very long way away, or with some fantastic excuse in your back pocket about how you were on the way to the off-licence when an old lady who was skateboarding down the road fell off and before your very eyes trapped her gusset in the grating of a drain and while you waited for the fire brigade to arrive to cut her out it closed – then never come to dinner without bringing a bottle of wine.

Whatever you do, don't turn up empty-handed. Cooking, even getting food in from a takeaway, still takes time and effort. In some way a bottle also reduces the debt you're in to the host. It balances the mutual obligation. Although you might not actually want to take wine if you know that the person cooking is a bit of an enthusiast and is likely to have chosen particular wine to go with the food. Don't mutter 'pretentious' under your breath, now. Just hope that they do know what they're talking about and take flowers or chocolates instead. And if you're a host who does choose wine carefully to go with the food, don't just silently squirrel the present of wine away: tell them what you're doing and that you want them to taste the stuff you've decided to open already because it goes with what you've cooked. Generally in France, Spain, Italy and Portugal avoid taking wine. It can be misconstrued as a sign that you think they won't have any already.

Flowers, too, can be difficult, though only because they mean all sorts of different things in different countries. In eastern Germany they can signal romantic intentions. Chrysanthemums are often placed on graves and, while for some friend's cooking that might be a symbol entirely pregnant with correctness, it can cause upset; in Norway carnations are a definite symbol of death. But who'd dream of taking carnations anyway. Horrible things. In Bulgaria yellow flowers mean hatred. But, you know, most people aren't that sensitive. If you've gone to some trouble and cooked, then a present is a thank you for that. And flowers would be lovely.

Starting to eat

At the root of many rules about eating lies the intention to dictate a certain self-consciousness in diners about what they are doing. There are a whole set of rituals that begin dinners and discourage people from just chowing down without the host or hostess saying 'Eat'. We wait for permission. In Canadian summer camps, it is said, there is a game that they play. If an individual is guzzling quite oblivious to the rest of them, one of the others will do something daft like put their finger in their ear. Once the other campers realise this is not a precursor to one of those dreadful too-ra-ra-alay songs they start to join in one by one and insert their fingers aurally. Eventually the single-minded eater is the only one with his fingers still on his knife and fork and the others all then shout 'Pig'. This sounds not unlike the plot of *Lord of the Flies*, but I suspect Canadians shouting 'Pig' is probably a marvellously supportive exercise that carries with it a series of young-person-friendly social work support systems and some positive reinforcement exercises for the young stuffer.

Grace is not terribly common these days, but maybe we should revive my favourite pre-dinner ritual, which is Japanese. The Ainu, who live in the north-east of Japan, have ceremonial long moustaches which have lifters to prevent them getting dirty. They take these carved lifters and dip them in the sake or the soup and throw some of either on the floor. And they pray as they do it. If I didn't have carpets I'd make it compulsory in my house.

It's a peculiarity of manners that we go to great lengths, in all cultures, to prove to each other that we are capable of restraint and not driven simply by desires that are near-carnal. As with sex, food requires foreplay. And is far better for it.

Where people should sit

This drives people who are concerned with etiquette absolutely barmy, mainly because, if you're going to follow strict etiquette, you have to implement rules developed at Court throughout Europe over the last four centuries or so. You would have to make a series of frankly odd calculations about who is the most important guest at your table. This can eventually require a slide rule and plenty of homework. This functioned without that much fuss at Court because to a certain extent people knew their place. They knew their political status. They were pretty clear about their position in the flattery food chain. And if they got it wrong? Well, according to the French historian of etiquette Henri Brocher, writing in the 1930s, and I paraphrase his elegant French, Louis XIV was so petulant about it occasionally he just threw his sceptre out of the pram when people sat in the wrong place and left the table. Which meant that no one could eat. Spoilt brat! Ambassadors used to fight about precedence until the Congress of Vienna in 1814 came up with a jolly compromise. An ambassador's seniority at the Court at which she or he represents his or her country is solely determined by his or her length of service.

But which of us is that posh? And how many of us have people at our tables who worry about their seniority. It is only with the very old that it might be worth thinking about putting them in the traditional position of top man on the right of the hostess and top woman on the right of the host. And that's only because, being older, they might feel more traditional about it and that would make them feel more comfortable. I have a preference for splitting up partners and stopping them sitting next to each other, but only because couples tend to behave like smug marrieds given the chance, gossiping privately and sharing little whispered *billets-doux*. This defeats the purpose of eating together. If they want to do that, they should go out for a romantic dinner alone and not bother the rest of us. And, secondly, if you part couples at the dinner table at least they've got something to talk about when they get home. But the rest of the time we should sit our guests where we think they'll have the best fun. As for seating people (or even asking people in the numbers that would make this possible) man, woman, man, woman round the table, just drag yourself into the twenty-first century love, he says a little sharply. You don't have to be gay – you could just be single – to find that a little odd these days.

Conversation

A friend's distinctly anti-papist uncle used to make the same joke to his nephew every time he sat down to a family meal. 'Mustn't talk about sex, religion or politics at the table, eh? Well, after Mass your father's mistress went and voted bloody Labour again.' It's such a bad joke. You can just about see that it's funny but it doesn't make you laugh. But it does hide a certain truth. Generally people think that meals together shouldn't be about arguments. The worst memories a lot of people have of their childhoods are the terrible fights their parents had at the table either with each other or with their children. At Christmas, fuelled by too much alcohol, the same uncle would apparently get so blotto that he'd eventually turn to his brother's wife, his by now very long-suffering hostess, and slur at her, 'You know, I never really liked you. I always thought he could do better.' She never took the bait.

Manners as we eat together are about handling the possible conflicts, which doesn't mean avoiding them. Be honest; what is there more worth talking about than sex, religion or politics? But we learn to disagree in what we have come to call a civilised manner, although we seem to have learnt to forget that skill pretty soon after a certain amount of alcohol. If you're the host, it's up to you to manage the situation. That's the point of manners. Don't let the guests meta-phorically, or worse literally, try to kill each other. One family I know has a phrase it uses when one of them sees a finger poised over the nuclear button in an argument. It's a diversionary tactic, developed to signal to the rest of the family that the cavalry is needed to head off a potential massacre. 'What a beautiful bird the peacock is' one of them will say. And in the hiatus caused by the inanity of this remark, a subtle change of direction is supposed to be engineered. Of course, firstly it's such a daft thing to say that it rarely diverts people from fighting about the rights and wrongs of abortion or hunting or whatever. But more useless than that, now all the family know what was supposed to be a secret sign; the minute they hear someone say it they all stop what they are talking about, thinking 'oh goody, a fight'. And they join in the argument. Volatile as they are as a family, though, they are actually pretty good at diffusing major conflicts into enjoyable intellectuals rucks. Which would be good manners at the table.

Farting, belching, elbows on the table and other bugbears

Many of us come from families who will always think that farts are funny. We announce them proudly and pronounce heartily on their quality and resonance. We generally behave around them with the lack of inhibition which is in complete contrast to the taboos that have built up around bodily functions since Erasmus's day. The bourgeoisie tend to be very delicate about farting, belching, weeing and pooing. Though farts have a great deal more latitude than the other three. They are a comic staple, for instance. One of the most celebrated *Punch* competition winners showed a cartoon of three Edwardians in *a* posh sitting room with the caption supplied by a reader: 'How dare you fart in front of my wife!' To which the culprit responds, 'I'm so sorry. I didn't know it was her turn.'

But funny or not, farting, it should be said, is pretty natural. There is some evidence to suggest that in medieval times men who couldn't pass a ripping bubble of gut wind were called weaklings. Sissies. Perhaps predictably in a culture that so reveres the tuba, there's even a German word for someone who can't produce a decent *pumpf*, he's a *pimpf*. Erasmus was very strict in his advice, in this case about behaviour in church: 'Fidgeting in one's seat, shifting from side to side, gives the appearance of repeatedly breaking wind or of trying to do so. The body should therefore be upright and balanced.' But he also says when you want to fart, go for it: 'There are some who lay down the rule that a boy should refrain from breaking wind by constricting his buttocks. But it is no part of good manners to bring illness on yourself while striving to appear polite. If you may withdraw, do so in private. But if not, then in the words of the old adage, let him cover the sound with a cough.'

These days lots of people are not so sanguine. Farts are a cause of enormous embarrassment. George Carlin, the American comic, made the point that when two people are in a lift and one of them farts, everybody knows who did it. Farts make some people's toes curl with shame. They try and hide their own and ignore other people's. So if you witness a fart, the kindest thing to do is to ignore it, even when it smells as if there's a badger down there. Because you never know how embarrassed the person might be. Unless, of course, you were in the company of Le Pétomane, the famous fartiste of the Moulin Rouge in the 1880s, who farted sensationally for a living. He had in his repertoire every fart, from the delicate 'bride on her wedding night' to the thunder of a cannon. He could produce four tones naturally – do, re, mi and the octave do, though not quite with Julie Andrews's crisp delicacy, and his act produced the kind of hysteria in an audience that required the presence of nurses in the theatre to tend to those overcome with laughter. It is best to assume, however, if only as insurance, that while we may laugh to the point of tears at farting in a theatrical context, close up most people are to be presumed embarrassed until found enthusiastic about it. So be discreet when they fart and apologetic, if it's appropriate to mention it at all, when you do.

Curiously, perhaps, most of us have never felt the same robustness about belching, although there are far more cultural reasons to be delighted by it. There are a number of countries in which it is regarded as not merely okay but a positive compliment. In Arab and Persian culture slurping tea, drinking coffee with loud sighs of satisfaction and belching at the end of the meal are all noisily appreciative gestures. Whereas to do that in a European or American house is thought terribly boorish.

The curious thing about burping is that it is acceptable, in fact heartily encouraged, in babies. It's like walking. Parents spend hours and hours teaching you to walk when you're a child. But once you can, they put you in a playpen or tie you into a harness in order to stop you. Burping is the same. You're encouraged to burp till you get on to solids. But we have developed a prohibition on burping which pretty much stands today. What sets it apart from farting in Britain may be because the British find bottoms irresistibly funny. We love to laugh at the taboo being broken. One of the funniest things Lady Rumpers says in Alan

Bennett's play *Habeas Corpus* is, 'When I hear the word arse, I know which way the wind is blowing.' To fart is to break a taboo to such an extent that it produces gales of cathartic laughter. Burping doesn't quite carry with it the same fabulous release of tension.

Children at the table

In order to rescue children from the tyranny of adults, we seem to have gone from the 'seen-and-not-heard' school of how children should behave at the table to the I'll-take-you-to-the-European-Court-of-Human-Rights-if-you-don't-let-me-play-my-drum-kit-during-lunch' school of encouragement of little Tarquin's potential. Okay, we all know children, lots of them, who are a complete delight to eat with. But there are others one just wants to eat. Preferably after they have been boiled in oil.

When children run riot at meals or in restaurants, let's face it, it's a nightmare for the rest of us, whether we've got children or not. From the moment they are born, no matter whether they look like Winston Churchill or Mother Teresa, their parents think they look like Helen of Troy or a little Greek god.

Which is as it should be. But from the moment they can speak, no matter how unpleasantly behaved they are, their parents also think that they do lttle else but drop pearls of delight into the world. This is not good. In all cultures meals are where children learn the rules of their parents, of adults. So as they in turn get older, and closer to being adults, society permits them more freedom at the table as they can be trusted to keep to what they've learnt. That's the classic anthropological thesis. And it's probably true. But its success for the rest of society depends on the parents bothering to teach the kids, otherwise the theory doesn't do us that much good.

We have all been to Spain, Italy and France enough now, particularly to the rural parts, and observed with amazed pleasure that the learning process around meals seems so much more self-conscious in the presence of several generations. Implicitly the social values of sharing and behaving in a group of people are learnt through the rituals of eating together. Their hot climates, perhaps simply because they allow more playing together outside, develop in kids a greater sense of shared space. Eating together in large groups is simply easier outside. This doesn't feel like a myth, either. It's commonplace to say that kids in those countries are treated with more respect. By the same token they are also expected to behave with more responsibility in public. An Australian friend who lives in France took her sister and nieces from Melbourne out to lunch at her local café in Toulouse last year. The girls immediately started to clamber under the table and treat the restaurant as a climbing frame in the playground. When gentle pleading made as much impact as King Cnut did on the waves, my friend told them rather testily to sit down, adding as if it implied some kind of ill-defined sanction – a special kiddie-portion guillotine perhaps – 'This is France'. Later one of the children was overheard telling her father, 'In France, Dad, It's illegal to go under the table.' Would that we could legislate that easily for kids to behave at meals or for parents to enforce it. It's not just being a stampy-foot adult to say this but there's an anthro-pological truth about it. Kids need to be taught manners. Sartre got it wrong. Hell is not other people. When they run amok in restaurants or at the table, hell is other people's kids.

5

—ᘯ—

CONVERSATION

A friend of mine used to chair an EU scientific colloquium in the days when there were just fifteen members of Europe. The convention at those meetings was that at the start you voted on the language to be used. Over ten years the result was always the same: thirteen for English, one against and one abstention. No prizes for guessing who cast the vote against and who was the abstainer. Against? Of course. The French. *Naturellement*. And the abstention? The Brits. Because we couldn't possibly impose . . . no goodness me, if people would like to speak English then that's, of course, marvellous . . . and it makes it jolly convenient for us, I know, which is all rather embarrassing, but absolutely fine if that's what people want. But you know, if you'd like to vote again, then do feel free . . .

We are, you will remember, the only people in the world who apologise when someone else stands on our foot.

When we Brits think about manners in conversation we are very conflicted between bluntness and indirectness. The cult of plain speaking, which we admire in some circumstances, is at war with the style of our politeness, where what is thought to be good manners clothes our desires in all sorts of prevaricating expressions. Good manners distances us from the immediate satisfaction of our needs. Which is not an unusual function of manners. And we have a particularly British way of doing it. We are far less likely to approve of someone saying, 'Give me the salt' than saying, 'Could you possibly pass me the salt?' 'Would you mind terribly . . .?' Would it be a bore if . . .?' And when we are being truly, madly, deeply, ridiculously and wonderfully, self-denyingly British, we say, possibly with a slight cough, hoping in a bizarre moment of paradox that they will not want the salt themselves, but notice that we do: 'Erm. Would *you* like the salt?' Because if not I'd like to rub it into the wound of national self-deprecation, if you don't mind.

Other cultures are distinctly not like this. Scandinavians find this indirectness quite impossible. They just ask for things. And we slightly recoil at their bluntness and add it to our resentment at their blondness. But they are bugeyed at our circuitousness. When I went to Moscow it was 'International Shut A Door in a Tourist's Face' Week. In their daily exchanges the Russians seem to employ a kind of confrontational bluntness. You also find a disarming directness in the language of many of the Hakka Chinese people in Britain. At the Dumpling Inn in Macclesfield Street in Soho – which is mainly worth mentioning not so much for the food, which is fine, but for the bit of trivia that it is next to the door that was the exterior of the flat where George Segal and Glenda Jackson had their affair in *A Touch of Class* – my father asked the owner what happened downstairs. And he replied, 'You want to know. You go see.' He wasn't being in the least rude. In fact, the opposite. Translated into silly Brit that is, 'How kind of you to ask. And if you'd like to have a look downstairs, please feel free when you've got a moment.' Until we realised that was what he meant we were a bit taken aback. Tarzan may have introduced himself with now legendary curtness when he said, 'Me Tarzan, you Jane', but if he'd been true to his provenance as the lost child of the British aristocrats Lord Greystoke and Lady Alice, he'd probably have said, 'Frightfully nice to meet you. Um, I'm Tarzan. And I think you said your name was – Jane? But I might have got that wrong'. Maybe in the next remake Hugh Grant will play him.

We have developed a particular way in the language of being well-mannered. It's not that surprising, because if we British can barely express our emotions when they're at their highest peak how on earth can you expect us to risk rejection when we ask for the salt. John Mortimer once told me in an interview the way to write a British love scene. The first person looks over the table into the other one's eyes and says, 'Tea?' And the other looks back and says, 'Yes'. And the cup is filled. Well, that's pretty much it. Although I know that you have already pictured the tea being poured as they look into each other's eyes and it has overflowed into the saucer and then into the lap of the pourer. And there is much comic flapping just to make sure that no American turns up and starts to take it all too seriously and gush sentimentally. However, if you did want to go the whole romantic hog – I am not sure that hog is quite the right word – you add the following exchange: 'Sugar?' 'Oh, yes.' It's done now. No swelling of chords in the background can equal the tumescence of their love.

This is all jolly larky stuff, but there is a serious undertow. What many people identify as going wrong in conversation in many of our encounters with each other in Britain at the moment is that people are not bothering with the softening of their needs. They are just being too direct. They are invading what people think is their personal space by just starting conversations willy-nilly. And once they've got going they are playing fast and loose with the directness of expression. The dance with words that we have come to identify with manners and our way of easing our interaction has become intermittent. In fact, people are more and more in effect just saying, 'Oi, you, give me the bloody salt. Now!' Or even more effing forcefully than that. And we don't like it. Or rather, would you mind terribly if it stopped?

While we are nervous of plain speaking and we think it rude, we are, of course, too polite to point it out. Instead we play out a pretence that we rather like folksy, 'real' people who speak their mind, call a spade a spade, come right out with it and so on, probably because we think that it exercises our egalitarian muscle. (And in Britain, I fear, we each have only one of those.) My mother once visited her new neighbour in Wiltshire, a very wizened small, old woman who looked a little like a walnut on casters. As my mother sat down, the first thing Mrs Weaver said, jabbing her finger towards next door and presumably in the direction of my father, was, 'Oi hear you're 'is second wofe' (please note the phonetic Wiltshire spelling to emphasise the folksiness of this anecdote), to which my mum replied, 'Actually, he's my second husband.' Or more correctly in posh: 'Ectually, he is my scnd hsbnd.' 'Oh yaas,' said Mrs Weaver, 'oi've 'ad some uv those.' And then she added with an unsavoury wink and in a deadly serious tone of voice, 'Oi 'spect you did away with the furst one. You posh people don't divorrrce 'em, do you?'. Now, it may not have been a direct accusation of murder, but on the face of it it was a little bold for a first meeting. However, in the family we all put it down to quaint rural plain speaking and speculated quietly, in our own middle-class way and certainly not in her presence, about the fact that she'd had three husbands all of whom had died. We never called the police. She also once cooked a very light custard for my mother, and said as she gave it to her, 'Oi cooked you this cos ur a bit faaat.' There is a sort of charm in there somewhere.

What we find difficult with plain speaking is not so much that it happens but when. The more someone is a stranger, the more indirect we are with them. The difference between friends and strangers is crucial when you are talking about manners. In Britain we spend a lot of time and cultural effort on how we behave with strangers, only to chuck it all in the bin of familiarity when it comes to our friends. To whom we are cheeky, blunt, sarcastic and, yes, even rude. And it just makes us closer. Friends by and large work out their own rules on how to treat each other. But with strangers we need to be more careful. It is a risk to behave like we would to a mate. Especially when you don't know who they are, where they come from or anything about them. So we negotiate the distance between, and ignorance of, each other by being polite. Manners put the unfettered expression of our needs and opinions under a degree of self-discipline. By reducing even the possibility of hostility, we have an easier time getting through life. Politeness in conversation negotiates the complexities of modern living, and transforms the potential violence and hostility of disagreement and conflict into ease with each other. Which is a posh way of saying, make the effort to be less blunt with people as soon as you meet them and you'll find that they will enjoy you more.

The contrast between how we treat friends and how we approach strangers in conversation couldn't be more extreme. It is in some ways quite bizarre in Britain how much we tease and torment our nearest and dearest. We seem to earn the kind of permission with them in private that in the public arena we only see with comedians, particularly drag artists, or ventriloquists. They play a similar game with the boundaries of politeness only with their audiences who are complete strangers. And the ruder they are the more we love it. Lots of comics do it but the outrage seems more explosive and hilarious as Dame Edna or Lily Savage viciously send people up, offloading the responsibility from Barry Humphries and Paul O'Grady on to their characters. Even odder, the more appallingly a ventiloquist's puppet behaves to someone in the audience, the more we squeal with delight. But the puppet is made of wood. We know it's the ventriloquist talking even if his lips don't move. And we delight in the social anarchy that is ignited by him crashing through taboos. Right then we all want to be the puppeteer. We are fascinated by what would happen if we were that rude but we don't dare. However, all this happens in the controlled context of theatre. Or with banter and teasing in a framework of friendship. As much as we're delighted by the opportunity to drive through our social prohibitions when we watch comedy, we're rightly appalled when it happens in the uncontrolled environment of the street.

Between friends, banter and apparent rudeness are often ways of expressing deep attachment. You hear friends explaining to people who don't know them that they can only be so rude to each other because they love each other. And we do love a brilliant barb. We don't necessarily regard them as bad manners. In fact, we retell the best ones constantly. Who was rude to whom. And oh, how we laughed. In reported speech, of course, we don't experience the embarrassment of the target. When you tell a good anecdote at a dinner party to some extent you excuse yourself from the responsibility of causing that. Even if you actually did. Humiliation is always bad manners. But we don't necessarily disapprove of the report of it. We think wit is a joy. When Blackwell, the American designer, described Elizabeth Taylor in one of her larger phases as 'looking like two small boys fighting under a mink blanket', we worshipped him. We can almost forgive the dreadful Sir Thomas Beecham his bullying manner for calling Herbert von Karajan 'a kind of musical Malcolm Sargent'. To say (sadly anonymously) that 'if white bread could sing, it would sound like Olivia Newton-John' gets close to genius.

This kind of wit is a game because it's about the playing not the winning. And it is not a game of solitaire. It is verbal copulation. It thrives through conversation and is partly a way of working off our competitive and aggressive instincts when it is socially undesirable to hit or hurt each other. Blunt insults are just bruising, but cloaked in wit, even when you're the target, they can just about live up to Mary Poppins's prescription of the spoonful of sugar. At work people banter; many families tease constantly. The jokiness of the way we talk to each other is a form of manners in that often it masks the direct expression of emotion.

Banter makes our affection manageable. It makes what we feel easier to say and easier sometimes to hear. But banter has to exist within rules.

As they used to say on TV, don't try this at home. Unless you're pretty confident. We have a very capricious attitude to those that would be funny. We love it when they are. But as Mrs Patrick Campbell said of Tallulah Bankhead, 'Tallulah is always skating on thin ice. Everyone wants to be there when it breaks.' As suddenly as we start to laugh, we can have a sense of humour failure and draw the line. People step over it constantly. And the difficult thing is that it is not static. It's a question of judgement. Some people are more easily offended than others. So someone who has a limited sense of humour can regard your flippancy as far too intimate. You can be a bit fresh with some stuffed shirt who thinks they're a bit too important for that, although in that case it's a toss up about who's being ruder if they react badly and slap you down. Maybe they should have had the grace to pass over it. We all know the dead moment, though, when someone oversteps the mark, when something was supposed to be funny, but it just wasn't. Although misjudgement and bad manners in conversation are two different things. If you overstep the mark with someone you don't know, apologise immediately. And if you are the recipient accept the apology equally fast.

Anyone can make a mistake about other people's feelings. Bad manners is not to recognise that it was just that.

We are talking about social hiccups here, but far deeper conflicts do happen in conversation. Then we do have to find a way not just of getting over them but of resolving them. It's useful to try and negotiate to avoid this happening. Approaching strangers with a lesser degree of bluntness, or our elders or just people we don't know terribly well, not always expressing the fullness of our opinions immediately, or sometimes ever at all, are the kind of restraint for the greater social good that manners might dictate. We experience this most often with political or generational differences. We've all sat round the table when Granny has said something fantastically reactionary about immigration, but who's going to change her at eighty-three? There are old friends who simply agree not to talk about the war in Iraq because it'll bust them apart. You may refrain from talking as fruitily about sex as you might normally if there are nuns at the table.

But the British are better at avoiding conflict than at dealing with it. We'd rather look away than look somebody in the eye. It's interesting to see around the world how many traditional ceremonies there are for formal processes of reconciliation in other countries, sometimes between individuals and sometimes between communities and nations. I remember going to a conference in 2004 on Robben Island in South Africa organised by the Institute for the Healing of Memories. Its chair is a priest called Fr Michael Lapsley, who lost both his hands to a letter bomb posted to him, he suspects, by the South African Secret Service in 1990. He was and still is an ANC chaplain. He is a great promoter of healing through reconciliation. At this gathering there were South Africans talking about the Truth and Reconciliation Commission in all its glory and its faults. There was a woman from Western Samoa who described her island's traditional ceremony of forgiveness and reconciliation, which is called *ifgoa*, and the formal apology that the New Zealand Premier, Helen Clark, had made earlier that year for the colonial actions of her country. There were Rwandans, Kenyans, Vietnamese, all of whom described a rainbow of restorative rituals. East Timor has a Commission for Reception, Truth and Reconciliation and Chile has set up its own form of the same. Towards the end I was asked to say something about Britain. So I just said that we Brits had been listening in some awe to these descriptions of justice under an African tree, *ubuntu*, and a remarkable quiver of other concepts to symbolise and guide the process. In Britain we have none of these. In Britain our national characteristic is a kind of sullen resentment. We'd much rather hold on to a grudge. Take it out occasionally and burnish it.

We don't do reconciliation very well. We do lots of retribution. You can read that in the coverage of crime in the tabloids as they bay for the hunting down of child offenders and deny the possibility of a change for the better in the behaviour of criminals. Although on the apology front, political leaders have taken to issuing them like Santa handing out sweeties, apologising for a variety of British mistakes in the past, largely colonial ones. In 2004, the Queen was called on by the German newspaper *Bild* to apologise before her state visit there for the bombing of Dresden. But they're pretty empty gestures. It turns out that sorry is not the hardest word. In fact it's pretty easy. Politicians, albeit under pressure from a hungry press and successful pressure groups, pump them out like mints from a tick-tack dispenser. Apologies are quite what is needed when you stand on somebody's foot, or spill juice on their baby, if you parked in their space or didn't fold their bra when you undressed them. These are random small things for which apologies are thoroughly appropriate. But for the big things sorry is too small a word. With the bra *faux pas* you can probably get over it with a sorry. Or if you want to be terribly British, then a 'terribly sorry'. But if you bombed their country, or repressed their people or slung them falsely in gaol, more may be needed.

If manners are about our ability to live together, then in the way that we talk to each other they must encompass the much more difficult task of putting threatened relationships on a new footing. If you argue with a friend, if you insult someone you really like or love in an unguarded moment, if you dish out a spit of drunken venom or even, much more seriously, break the bonds of faithfulness with your partner, it'd be good manners to find a way to create a reconciliation. You can go on saying sorry but if you can't get them to accept it, then communication will close down.

So let's start at the difficult end of manners and conversation, with arguments, which conveniently begins with A.

ARGUMENTS

There are three kinds of argument.

The first is the kind you have in the pub, which we'll take to include any verbal fisticuffs that are a laugh and keep to the no-offence-on-either-side-rule. They can be one to one, but they're more difficult to keep within the parameters if they are. They are better in groups. They can get as ferocious as you like. But they must never get personal. Insults may be hurled but they must never be *ad hominem*. And they are not characterised by what you're arguing about. It is possible to ratchet up the temperature and pace as easily in a row about the rules of marbles as it is about Chelsea or Arsenal or capitalism and socialism. But the unwritten principle is that 'no animals are to be hurt in the making of the film'. Some people will say that woman don't argue like this, only men. Well, firstly let me say that that is a tremendous subject for just such an argument. And secondly can I say, bollocks. As you would in the pub. And you mustn't take offence. I didn't mean it. It was just an example.

Women love this kind of argument; they just don't shout as much as men. The Irish are best at it. It's the *craic*. They can argue all night long, stand on chairs, bellow, scream, quote poetry and sing. No one is actually trying to convince anybody of anything. The fun is in the verbal volleying. And in the morning absolutely no one remembers anything of what was said. This marvellously enables the whole thing to happen all over again. Which does begin to make you wonder about the Peace Process. Israelis argue at the drop of a hat too. An American architect I know went on a site visit to Jerusalem with a number of high-ranking government officials when he was developing a very significant project there. He thought it had all gone rather well until they got to the cars to drive back into the centre of town. At which point an enormous argument broke out in Hebrew, which he doesn't understand. He started to worry. He thought they might come to blows. It looked like his project might grind to a sudden halt as it fell between the cracks of what was clearly a volcanic dispute. In fact they were arguing about which car should give him a lift back to the office.

Arguments like this often lead to sex, more booze, another argument and usually forgetting what you were shouting about in the first place. There is only one rule apart from not taking these kinds of arguments seriously. The first person to mention Hitler loses. Not, of course, that it's about winning. These arguments are there for a purpose. We are picking fleas out of each other's fur.

They appear to be highly conflictual, but they are conversely, of course, about getting closer to each other. We take free rein to say things we don't necessarily believe. We are rolling around in the hay of conversation with each other, exercising our conversational love muscles. Accusations are levelled from time to time that we have lost the art of conversation because we don't talk about anything serious. And they always add 'any more', as if in the streets of pre-war London they talked of little else but the loss of the gold standard and the changing face of international relations in Europe. We decidedly haven't lost the art. We don't have to be Whistler and Wilde *bon mot*ing into extra time to feel the pleasure and purpose of just chewing the fat. The manners of this kind of conversation, which deliberately keep it from being really serious, therefore allow almost anybody to join in because there is little apparently at stake.

The second type of arguments are formal ones and happen between politicians, the professionally prejudiced pundits who appear on shows like *The Moral Maze* and colleagues at work. They are not so much arguments as stags rutting in a clearing. Men (usually, but not always) strut at the House of Commons Dispatch Box, the studio table or the office desk and mainly compare the size of their penises. With these arguments the rules vary. In British politics, the House of Commons clings to what it calls tradition and the rest of us think of as pantomime. Top hats are worn from time to time, as are crowns. Everybody has to call everybody else the Honourable Member when in fact they hold each other in very little honour and do indeed mostly think of each other as members. If you get my drift. The point of these arguments, as with the set pieces on radio and TV, is not to convince anyone but to set out a position. The rules are by and large made up of specific etiquettes, which you don't need to know unless you are one of these people. And if you are one of these people, you'll know them already. They're not hard. Insults are permitted. In fact sneering is a requirement. The degree to which you can get away with them is judged by the public witnessing the fight rather than any of the participants, although at the same time we are all completely partisan in these matters. So any insult hurled by our man or woman is a direct hit and one by the other side's is a foul. It's like football. The ref only needs glasses when the other team scores an off-side goal. These arguments have reached the pinnacle of their art with broadcast political interviews which consist almost entirely of tripwire journalism. A politician could announce the name of her cat and the presenter would pick a fight about it. This corrodes manners because, despite the rules, it helps no one to get along with each other or understand each other and operates as a terrible model to anyone listening.

Its most damaging effect is on the debates the rest of us want to have about subjects that matter to us. It gives the impression that what is important about arguing is to win. Well, in the hostile polka of politics, you need to appear to do so. There are votes at stake, after all. But in reality we are rarely convinced to change our mind completely by a single debate. And certainly not immediately. When did you last have a eureka moment watching *Question Time*?

So I am about to wave my plaits in a Heidi-like manner and lay myself open to accusations of futile utopianism. But here's the proposition. If we get anything out of serious arguments with each other, it's a shading of our opinion, a nuance, a slight shift, a bit of information that might make us reconsider our view. Importantly in discussions the different points of view together create an entirely new one. You'll think I'm wearing sandals if I quote a traditional Native American proverb referred to in William Isaacs' book *Dialogue*. And you might rightly point out that the Native Americans didn't do terribly well at surviving the onslaught against them. But there is a saying in some of those cultures, 'You talk and talk until the talk starts.' Dialogue is created by the two Greek words *dia* and *logos*. Dia means 'through' and *logos* means 'word' or 'meaning'. It also has an older root in the sense of 'gather together'. But, whatever the roots and the Greek, and whatever the Native American proverbs, for the best justification for a different way of arguing we can look to the way that we enjoy talking with each other the most. And this is when we genuinely discuss, adapt our thinking, refine our views and enable ourselves to reach conclusions together, however small, that lead us to act. The best manners in an argument about something serious is to listen. Really listen. Lay yourself open to the possibility of a change in your view. I told you I was going to wave my plaits. This means that when somebody is talking, don't think of what you are going to say next, rather, concentrate on what they are saying now. It will mean that you don't say what you were going to say irrespective of how the discussion has moved on. It often means acknowledging what someone else has said, even if you don't agree with it, by telling them that what they have said is interesting or important. Because that can disarm the tone from being confrontational and turn the conversation to being far more collaborative. The best-mannered way of listening may be to give the other person more confidence to speak, even if that means telling the tiniest of white lies. But who said that having manners meant telling the truth?

The third kind of argument is where you lose it completely. You hurl yourself off your trolley, fuelled by jealousy, rage, alcohol, stress, hurt, upset, sadness or a real wound. You are out of control. These are arguments we usually have with people we love. And we will say things that we may regret for ever, that are true or untrue, that flatten everybody in the surrounding area against the wall. We will accuse the people we love the most of doing and saying things we wouldn't in an emotionally sober moment accuse people we hate the most of even thinking of doing or saying. There are no rules in these arguments.

In such circumstances, all you can do is learn how to apologise.

Now, as I said, in Britain we find this all a bit difficult. But if you look at the rituals in all those countries and tribes I mentioned earlier they follow a pattern. It might help to understand what that is. To find a future with each other, these rituals all demonstrate how important it is to listen to each other's experience of the hurt. At all costs this is not about justifying what you did. By all means explain why you did what you did, but in neutral terms. If you were wrong you must make restitution. In many of these cultures this is symbolic, and it can seem a bit odd to anyone outside the culture. In fact, when I say 'a bit odd' see under 'British understatement'. For instance, in Western Samoa, where the anthropologist Penelope Meleisea has written extensively about forms of reconciliation and they are referred to in judgements in their Supreme Court, those representing the perpetrators of a crime sit outside the house of the victim with a valuable piece of cloth on their head all night, holding a bunch of sticks in one hand and a stone in the other. This symbolises the fact that they are prepared to be thrown into the cooking oven like an animal and thus demonstrates their humility. In the morning they are invited in by the victims and speeches of apology and reconciliation are made, gifts are accepted, which is a sign that forgiveness is granted, and people move on. We don't have anything that remotely resembles this. And I'm not suggesting you start sitting outside your neighbour's house with a scarf on your head if your child trampled his rose bushes. But we simply don't have any rituals of reconciliation in Britain.

Every morning at 5.30 on Radio Four they play the BBC Radio 4 'UK Theme', a medley representing the four countries. If you're of a trainspotting or stamp-collecting mentality you might like to know that they are 'Rule Britannia', 'Londonderry Air', 'What Shall We Do With The Drunken Sailor', 'Greensleeves', 'Men Of Harlech', 'Scotland The Brave' and 'Early One Morning'. Which means that in among the gentler wishes of 'Londonderry Air' – 'Would God I were the tender apple blossom, That floats and falls from off the twisted bough' – the Radio Four listener wakes to the bellicose Scots going on about how 'high may your proud standards gloriously wave' and, after 'rooting the native oak', 'Rule, Britannia!' spends a number of verses fighting off 'each foreign stroke' and belligerently refusing to be slaves. In Western Samoa they wake to the traditional music of reconciliation, 'The Honourable Ve'ehala'.

In Britain we have judicial inquiries and we have family huffs. We make clumsy, ineffective bureaucratic attempts at mediation in divorce. And we have no idea how to move forward from an argument other than a mumbled apology. Or worse. Flowers. And it would have had to have been a very big bouquet indeed if the Queen had decide to say it with flowers to Dresden.

If you want to try and heal the wound, what is worth taking away from the far greater hurts of those involved in bigger conflicts on the world stage is that hearing each other is more important than justifying yourselves.

BLESS YOU

I only put this in because the British are so pathetic about talking to strangers. Only a Brit can sit on a twenty-three-hour flight to Australia and not even say hello once to their neighbour. And you're thinking, with darn good reason. Why would I want to start a conversation with someone with whom my only bond is through the crapshoot of airline seating assignment? I might as well look up some of the other people who won a tenner in that week's Lottery and move in with them. Well, the great thing about somebody sneezing is that it gives you the opportunity to say 'Bless you'. You smile at each other and for a second there is a fleeting bond in a disaggregated world. It's a little delight. And for a moment it conquers that British reserve.

The long-established myth about why you say 'Bless you' is that when you sneezed you either blew the evil spirit out, in which case you were to be congratulated, or your soul was in danger of escaping and so you needed the blessing by way of protection. While looking for different cultural variations on this, I came across a charming Japanese chat room that had set up a conversation about sneezing. A Tokyo teacher of Japanese as a foreign language noticed that when one of her students sneezed an American or European fellow student would bless them. So she asked in the chat room for students to write and tell her what other customs were around the world. She was rather sweetly worried that a Westerner would feel upset if they sneezed in Japan and no one said bless you, which they wouldn't.

In Japan they typically have a very well and elegantly organised system to interpret sneezing: one sneeze means praise, two criticism, three disparagement and four, they say, means you have a cold.

However, curiously in such a ritualised and polite society there appears to be no obligation to say bless you or thank you. Which means they are missing out on the possibilities of what happens in Spain, where they also count the number of sneezes: one you say, '*Salud*' (Health), two, '*Salud y dinero*' (Health and money) and three times, '*Salud y dinero y amor*' (Health and money and love). There the sneezer responds, '*Gracias*' (Thank you). If by any chance the person sneezing is Iranian you might like to try, '*Afiyat bashe*', which means, 'I wish you good health'. And you'll know they're Iranian because they will reply '*Elahi shokr*', which means 'Thank God for health'. In Brazil when someone sneezes they sometimes say, '*Saude*', which again means, 'Health'. And often older people say, '*Deus te ajude*'; either way the sneezer says, 'Amen'. In Yugoslavia you can try, '*Na zdravlje!*', Poland, '*Na zdrowie*', and in Lithuania, '*I Sveikata*'. They all mean 'Health'. In India it's just bad luck to sneeze. Germans, Jews and intellectuals from Hampstead say '*Gesundheit*'. The French say, '*A tes souhaits*', which roughly translates as 'May your wishes come true', and if you know them very well you can say '*A tes amours*', which you can translate yourself. A Korean friend said that they just copy the sneezer by giving an onomatopoeic '*Eichi*'. But only if you are very close to them, otherwise you ignore it.

According to Opie and Tatem's *A Dictionary of Superstitions*, the first literary mention of sneezing is in Pliny's *Natural History* of AD 77: 'Why is it that we salute a person when he sneezes, an observation which Tiberius Caesar, they say, the most unsociable of men, as we all know, used to exact, when riding in his chariot even?'

Don't ask why. The point is just do it. It shows that you're human.

CHAT ROOMS

People behave appallingly in chat rooms. For those of you who don't use them, just a little briefing. You can talk about pretty much anything to pretty much anybody on the internet. This is both astonishing and unbelievably scary. Most of us take quite a lot of care choosing the people we mix with. In internet chat rooms you can feel like you're in the cyber equivalent of the bar in *Star Wars*. Nonetheless, if you're in a chat room about gardening, model trains, ancient history, pressing wild flowers or beekeeping you've got little to fear except extreme boredom and typed assault by overenthusiasts. You probably popped in with a casual inquiry about whether anyone knows whether to plant forsythia on a north-facing wall. And you get accosted for hours by some earnest plant lover sending you messages.

However, saving your blushes, since the internet links people across the world around common interests, most chat rooms involve either *Star Trek* or masturbation. Or, in the case of DrSpockIwantyounow.com, both. And the names of the different rooms are pretty specific in the dating and sex chat sites. So don't go into one and then complain afterwards that you didn't know what you were letting yourself in for. A chat room on a dating site called 'Donkeys' shouldn't hold any surprises. The great thing about this is that you are completely in control. In the last resort you can just log off.

However, if you stick with it, once inside the site you can choose to go into a room, and once in a room can either chat with everyone in a free-for-all, the level of which is usually only slightly above amoeba, or you can choose to start a private conversation with one individual who, for whatever reason, you fancy talking to. This is where the trouble starts. They haven't asked to talk to you. In one sense, for them it's like being sat in the pub and the person at the next table just striking up a conversation. You've just barged into their life entirely without any kind of permission. But equally you've made yourself pretty vulnerable by showing interest. There are three courses of action normally taken by the recipient of such attention. They can say hello, be aggressive or ignore you. The first can lead to a conversation, a phone number, married bliss and children or the co-ownership of a small, white, fluffy poodle which you have groomed regularly at a shop called Doggy Style. All fine and dandy.

But aggression or silence are just rude. There is no reason to behave in a chat room any differently from the way you would in a bar, a club or on the street. If the approach was respectful or even neutral, the response should be equivalent. But we need conventions. One: don't pester someone. If there's no response, move on. Although I do remember Max Wall saying in that lugubrious way, born of the stoical pace of his climb to regain his true status as a genius: 'Don't give up immediately. If a joke doesn't work after fifteen or sixteen . . . years, then chuck it out.' But don't go on tapping them on the shoulder in a chat room.

Two: equally, if your shoulder is being tapped on, who needs to tell the truth to someone you haven't met, don't really want to meet, and, let's face it, definitely won't ever meet, if it's going to upset them? Is there any need to be brusque or hurt them? None whatsoever. So, as the *News of the World* would say, just make your excuses and leave. The best course is simply to say. 'Thanks, but I am a bit busy right now.' A bit of light research, which was an excuse for me to spend hours in chat rooms, reveals that it is a semi-accepted convention. So why don't we make it standard? How many times do we have to remind ourselves that manners are not about the truth or even the true expression of feelings? They're about making life easier for each other. And in this case you don't even have to look them in the eye, when you turn them down.

SWEARING

NOTE: If you don't like expletives, don't read this section. We've made a very grown-up decision not to use asterisks.

Chaucer thought that swearing was clever and fun and Ben Jonson's plays are full of 'fackins' and 'shit on your heads'. I only mention this because we know full well that there are all manner of precedents in literature for what is described in the technical language of linguistics as bilabial plosives and fricatives. And it's good to know there are technical terms because next time you lose it completely, don't worry. You didn't tell someone to piss off, you just let fly a bilabial plosive.

There have been attempts to stop swearing. In 1601 there was a parliamentary ban on coarse language. This was reasonably effective in published work although Robert Browning did slip through with the word 'twat' in 1848 in a poem called 'Pippa Passes'. But he mistakenly thought it meant a nun's habit. How sweet. But there is clearly no ban now. Swearing has reached epic proportions, and some people are very offended by it. It now appears in all sorts of places that it never used to. In literature, that freedom was won at the trial of *Lady Chatterley's Lover* in 1960 when the prosecuting counsel, Mervyn Griffiths-Jones, earned himeself a place in the annals of ridicule by brandishing the novel at the jury and famously demanding 'Is it a book that you would wish your wife or even servant to read?' And answer came there a very loud Yes!!! Although, to be honest, not many of us actually did. But we were very glad that we could. On TV Kenneth Tynan officially confirmed that London was swinging by saying the F-word for the first time in 1965. Do you have cable or satellite? You'll have noticed that he appears to have started something.

Swearing is divided into two kinds, blasphemy and obscenity, and of late one has waxed while the other waned. The ability of religious words to breach taboos in Britain has declined as Christianity has lessened its grip on the country. And, interestingly, a clue to the taboos of the future can probably be seen in the increasing unacceptability of racial epithets and particularly of words that offend against Islam.

Obscenity, or at least the use of the words that used to be thought obscene, has, on the other hand, risen. Undoubtedly tied up with the fact that we are far more open about sex in general, sexual swearing is now entirely commonplace. Before nouns, after nouns, in between nouns, in the middle of nouns and as every conceivable form of adjective and adverb it is used either to emphasise or express contempt. Yet in 1914 there was a national outcry when Eliza Doolittle just said Not Bloody Likely in Shaw's *Pygmalion*. The Bishop of Woolwich demanded the word be banned which, given the imminent global upheaval, does make you wonder just a bit whether he oughtn't to have been concentrating on more important matters. But ninety years or so on, the question of whether it is good or bad manners to swear has faded somewhat behind our level of immunity to it. It is interesting, just by the by, as Guy Browning pointed out, in Britain swearing tends to be, as they say on the VD clinic door these days, genito-urinary, whereas in Latin countries swearing is big on mothers, whores and illegitimacy and the Slavs use a lot of animals. It is easy to see the taboos being broken in South America, but it might make one a little nervous to take one's dog on holiday in Poland.

Whether we're verbally molesting people with reproductive human technology, calling our fellow mortals whores or virgins (and in different religions each is an insult) or implying that they are infertile orang-utans, we swear a great deal in private. Not all of us, but lots of us. And we tend to censor ourselves in public. Not all of us, but lots of us. The problem is that there is no real consensus about when and where swearing is acceptable. It certainly seems to be far more about the words themselves than the lewdness of their meaning. In sport we may only be world champions at rugby and curling, but we are the galactic superstars in the field of *double entendres*. In front of the most so-called respectable audiences, Kenneth Williams, and a million less successful imitators private and professional, or for that matter the prodigiously heterosexual Leslie Phillips, could put a salacious twist just on the word 'Hello' and, pregnant with illicit suggestion, reap howls of laughter from audiences. People may disapprove of swearing but we've still got pretty dirty minds. We find these insinuations hilarious because they are explicitly inexplicit.

In contrast – literal and generational – in an episode of the cartoon *South Park*, the writers deliberately used the word shit 162 times to make a point. And the young pop singer Eamon made a single called 'F**k It (I don't want you back)' which had thirty-three expletives in it, and he sold 550,000 copies. That's 18.1 million swear words out there. Although how curious is it to sing the words without the asterisks but censor them on the cover. That's like sticking your tongue out at a policeman. But behind his back.

At the other end of the scale was what happened in 1999 to a man called Timothy Boomer who came from Standish in Michigan. He lost his temper when his canoe overturned and his not unreasonable response was to let go a profanisaurus of invective and filthy words. Two children and their parents were within earshot and he was convicted under an 1897 Michigan law that prohibits cursing in front of women and children. He was sentenced to perform community service and either pay a $75 fine or spend three days in jail. Which we all can agree was perfectly ludicrous.

As the public and the private realm overlap more and more, of which the domestic gladiatorial spectacle of *Big Brother* stands as a tragic symbol, where and whether we can swear becomes increasingly unclear. It's no longer rebellious, yet it is still disapproved of by the majority of people in public. A middle-aged stagehand at the The City Varieties in Leeds said something to me in the wings one night early on in the new comedy boom in the eighties that perfectly illustrated this. He pointed to the comic on stage who'd just said 'balls' and said, shaking his head in disapproval: 'All this swearing is just bloody unnecessary.' And then he looked up at a stagehand in the flies who was carelessly carrying an iron weight overhead and shouted, 'Hey, fucking watch out with what you're doing with that fucking thing.'

Swear words range from violent to playful. They still have the power to shock and offend. And that's generally their function. So don't swear by way of attack. Don't shout obscenities at the ticket inspector or the traffic warden. You will. I will. We all will. But we shouldn't. It's a verbal act of violence. And we could probably do without it.

The best we can say about manners and swearing is, like drinking and driving, Think Before You . . . Because some people simply get very upset by it. You don't need to do it and, to be fair, they don't need to hear it. Although it's not always predictable who might take offence. And the most unlikely people can swear. I was at a wedding once and detailed to look after an elderly aunt of the groom. Small, elegant, with the kind of thick, clownish rouge that only eighty-five-year-olds can get away with, she was a beguiling combination of the wistful and the feisty. She must have been quite a looker, as people always said. To which she always replied 'I still am.' We met her in the lobby of the hotel at about 11.30, and she announced she'd like a drink. I said I thought the bar was closed. She looked at me as if I was a child in remedial woodwork, linked her arm through mine and, marching towards the bar, said, 'Of course it's open; don't be such a cunt.' Some of you will be offended, but I'm afraid I'm still laughing at the life in the old girl. But if you want a softer example, the first time the F-word was printed in the *Church Times* was in 2003 when Sister Helen Loder reported how, while out cycling, a youngster yelled at her that she was 'a fucking nun'. To which she replied gamely, 'One or the other. But I can't be both.' It was a perfect example of bluntness deflected by obliqueness.

HANDSHAKES AND KISSING

These are not strictly about conversation, so please forgive me for putting the section here. But they do often precede conversations and in fact even lead to them.

When you meet a friend, how do you normally greet them? Do you kiss, shake hands, mumble hello and trip over them as they try and kiss and you try and shake? Do you just get your glasses entangled? As a consequence of our national emotional constipation we need to get some order here. Handshakes have somewhat fallen into disrepute and unpopularity, whereas kissing is everywhere. Previously it was rather more simple. If you were British you didn't kiss; you just shook hands. Of course your mother kissed you. But, if you were a boy, your father did not once you had hit puberty and pacifism. Only girls carried on kissing. And then we joined Europe.

The French, Spanish, Italians, even the Dutch, kiss people whom they barely know. So, when you meet someone there is a warmth that acknowledges the encounter. In France and Spain the men shake hands, at almost any age, and the women kiss. Men kiss the women too and increasingly now the men. It's easy, delightful and, because everybody does it, it's comfortable in its predictability. It doesn't have to be formal either, but it just eases you into the conversation. At Sussex University library they did some research a while ago. The person at the book checkout touched every other borrower on the hand. Then by the door people were interviewed about the library service. There appeared to be a strong correlation between those who had been touched and how highly they rated the library service. If you go to the doctor and she doesn't at least feel the glands in your neck or take your pulse, you feel a bit cheated.

If we are going to re-invigorate the habit of hand-shaking we have to make one thing perfectly clear. The firmness of your shake is no indicator of the stiffness of your moral spine. Just because you crush bones and milk someone's hand with the force of a steel press, it doesn't really mean that you've got the strength of character of Winston Churchill. Many cultures, particularly African ones, don't shake hands like that at all. They have what can appear to be rather limp handshakes. Despite his remarkable moral stature Nelson Mandela's is a rather light handshake. (Regrettably this is not personal knowledge but gleaned from a friend.) With a handshake it is the contact that is important, not the fact that you can crack walnuts.

Kissing on the cheek

The British no longer back off kissing. But while you can shake everyone's hand, despite the fashionable patina that kissing bestows, you don't have to, and can't, kiss everyone. Even in the theatre. I once interviewed Elaine Stritch. At the opening party for her one-woman show she made her way down the stairs of the Savoy and headed for me. I was probably the last civilian she had seen, so presumably she had some vague idea that she had met me before. I leant forward to kiss her but she hissed in my ear. 'Don't kiss me. If everyone kisses me, it hurts.'

So, to sort out who to kiss and who not:

Air kissing – mwah, mwah

This is useful. It's occasionally pretentious, but it can be done by both men and women.

You may air kiss: other actresses/actors; aunts you do not like; anyone at a party; anyone you hate.

Never air kiss: anyone you want to sleep with; anyone you have slept with – unless it's a calculated insult; your partner, spouse

Friends – straight

Men have permission to kiss women and vice versa, even though they have never met them, simply because they are in some way attached to their partner (see also Friends – gay, below).

So, in a conventional heterosexual relationship: on saying hello, a man may kiss the new girlfriend of his best friend (or of just a close male friend); his girlfriend may kiss her too. A woman may kiss the new boyfriend of her best friend (or of just her close female friend); her boyfriend may kiss her best friend – but only in a chaste way; she will probably kiss her best friend as well. The boyfriends, however, will rarely kiss each other. Unless they are French.

Men traditionally have not kissed each other by way of greeting in Britain. In mainland Europe it is commonplace. With more and more gay men around the rules are changing. So:

Friends – gay

Everybody thinks that gay men like being kissed. It's partly very sweet because it's a way of acknowledging their presence in the world. Likewise straight women with lesbians. But not all gay people like it. I only kiss one particularly butch gay man I know in order to tease him because he shrinks like a child shying away from a mother with the corner of a spit-wetted hankie. Straight men kiss gay men with greater ease, mainly to show how jolly liberal they are. Though perhaps if they really want to do that they should start to kiss each other. And Australian gay men are so butch they don't kiss each other because they think 'it's bloody poofy'.

In general, though, gay men and women are more likely to kiss each other and therefore their friends. But be careful not to assume that just because someone's gay that automatically permits what some people feel is the overintimacy implied by kissing.

HOW TO START A CONVERSATION

There are, let's say, twenty-three double seats on the top of a bus. What do you do if you're British and the twenty-fourth person to get on? You have to share. Your Britishness has been fired up by the rally of pleases and thank yous when you boarded – minimum one please and four thank yous shared between you and the driver – and now you have to cope with being in bodily and maybe social contact with another passenger. Should you smile? Or will they be the nutter on the bus and take that as a sign to go on about their dole cheque not arriving, aliens invading Bognor or the tsunami being a portent of the Second Coming. And I know that you know that I am not making those up. I am not. Maybe I just have one of those faces that makes them want to talk to me. We will all eventually get to that comedic stage in our lives where we will start to tell people our age. No matter where we are, we will, out of the blue, announce to strangers that we are 'eighty-two you know'. I'm beginning to think I'll start early to ward them off. But the nutters on the bus and the old ladies at the bus stop are breaking a social taboo that we all recognise.

We are suspicious of uninvited conversation. To be fair, we don't know its motives. Women are understandably wary of the approaches of men on public transport. One witty friend of mine, having turned down the drunken advances of a man on the tube and been greeted with the accusation 'you a lesbian, then?' retorted 'you the alternative, then?' But quick-wittedness is not in everyone's armoury. And we do seem to have developed the ability to shut everybody else off and remain in our own private box. Even when we're crammed together in a tube in the rush hour the British manage to avoid eye contact with other people. Except to raise our eyebrows about Americans who are chatting on to each other and, worse, us, about how wonderful England is. It seems a limited number of people in Britain are able to look in an infinite number of different directions. There must be a mathematical equation.

In pubs we have very strict rules, but which, of course, are unwritten and therefore completely opaque to the uninitiated, about who you can talk to. For instance, as Kate Fox pointed out in *Watching the English*, the bar counter is the only place where it is socially acceptable to strike up a conversation *with a complete stranger*. This rule is sometimes extended to include tables very near the bar counter, and to the areas around the pool or bar-billiards tables or the dart board, but only to those *standing* near the players. If you watch people's behaviour like Kate Fox did, you'll see that these rules are very complex. The tables in the vicinity of these games are still private – unless those seated at them are *known to the players*, in which case they can comment and exchange banter. And then the rules for fellow regulars are much more relaxed than for strangers.

When we were students we used to go to a pub in Brighton where this middle-aged man used to berate us constantly for our political opinions. There we were arguing passionately for the emancipation of the working class, some of whom we had actually met, and one day he shouted at me, with not so much as a by your leave, 'I own things you know. Not like you little buggers. I own a yacht and a car and a house . . .' It's still one of the best insults anyone has ever hurled at me. 'I own things.' And just before the dawn of Thatcherism. If only we'd understood.

Even though he was a regular, it was fair enough for us to try and politely disengage from him and then, in some desperation, just ignore him. With this kind of unwanted intervention in our lives, we don't want to embark on conversations leading nowhere with people we'll never see again. They are, as Alan Bennett once called them, relationships 'of somewhat redundant intimacy'. But we owe it to each other not to pretend that we're all invisible to each other. Hence the value of saying 'Bless you'. And hence the need to make the effort to start conversations when we meet new people, strangers. One piece of advice that someone gave me once was always to say three things to a stranger at a party: (1) 'Hello I'm [name]; (2) 'I'm glad to be here because I've had a dreadful day'; (3) '. . . at work or, at home'. That way they know your name or recognise it because you went out with their cousin/ worked with their friend/appeared on *Crossroads* in 1968. They can ask you why your day was so bad, or they can wonder what you do at work or at home. You can vary the formula at will. Manners are a way of inviting people into a conversation (the 'Yes, and . . . No, but' rule is good here: 'I think Brad Pitt is a cutie'. 'Yes, and so is Johnny Depp.' 'I think Brad Pitt is a cutie.' 'Oh no, I think he's a dog, but Johnny Depp, on the other hand . . .'), carrying it on without resorting to violence and ending it with an attempt to lessen the possibilty of the other person feeling rejected. A useful one in that regard, particularly on the phone, is, 'I must let you get on.'

These may all seem like superficial social tricks. But manners in conversation are just a conscious effort to reaffirm our interdependence through talk, even if it's only fleetingly, at a party or just for a moment in the street. And these tricks help us to do it. It doesn't matter much what you're talking about because small talk and the pub argument are a triumph of form over content. They are grooming rituals. And in the greater scheme of things they are just one of the ways that we establish friendship. Manners, the rituals, are simply a path to the possibility of greater intimacy. They just untie your tongue and in tiny ways confirm our social bonds.

—⚍—

6

WORK

Using some very simple back-of-the-envelope maths you can work out the following. If you live till you are seventy-five you'll be on the planet for just over 650,000 hours. According to the Work Foundation two-thirds of people work more than thirty-five hours a week, so let's approximate it at thirty-seven hours. And let's assume that you work from the age of twenty-one till you retire at sixty-five and take a fortnight's annual holiday. (Are you keeping up?) I know that women can retire earlier, but, bear with this: it's only on the back of an envelope not the computer at the Office of National Statistics. If all that is the case, then, roughly speaking, you will work for 81,400 hours, which is about 12 per cent of your life. Whereas you will sleep for 29 per cent. Though, of course, if you have kids or live next to some of the students I have been neighbours with, that too will be nearer 12 per cent. The rest of the time you will spend going to the loo and trying to find a parking space. And you might fill another few thousand spare hours when you're not playing with your children by watching TV, eating out, horsing around on the pitch, sitting in the pub, making love or at the movies. And obviously the last two can be combined, if you like, in the interests of efficiency. And please extend the list at will.

But, despite it being only 12 per cent of our lives, paid work defines us, although we should nod in gracious awe at those mothers and carers who work all the hours they are sent and remain mainly unpaid. That work also defines them. Their back-of-the-envelope calculation looks rather different. Hours alive 650,000. Hours spent caring: most of them. But this chapter is about how we behave when we are engaged with paid work, either as colleagues or as customers. We can adapt Descartes from the seventeenth century and indulge in a bit of twenty-first century Cartesian dualism. These days it's not I think therefore I am, it's I work therefore I am. We're not even what we eat. We are where we commute.

One friend of mine is the only person I know who, when asked what he does, replies, 'I smoke'. He too has used the back of the envelope and worked out that he spends so much of his life dragging on a fag that in all honesty that is how he has to answer. But the rest of us respond when asked with anything from writer to bank clerk, road sweeper to chief executive, although there is a certain section of the British working population who, when they reply, are overcome by false modesty and say, 'I do a bit of consultancy'. This has rather more to do with their desire to stress that they don't really need to work like the rest of us than the fact that they're part-time. They aren't. They tend to be ferociously ambitious and climbing ever higher up the work food chain. You don't tend to get plumbers saying, 'I do a bit of ballcock and plunger' as much as you do merchant bankers admitting, 'I do a bit of banking'. Although there was a phase when actors said it a lot.

Between the wars there was a style for actors affecting a kind of insouciance about their work. Peter Ustinov used to tell a story about being in a play called *One of Our Aircraft Is Missing* in the early 1940s with a suave matinée idol called Hugh Williams. In rehearsal, Ustinov attempted to look casual and replicate the kind of languid 'I'm-just-smoking-a cigarette' style of acting made popular by Gerald du Maurier and other people who wore dinner jackets for a living. But Hugh Williams approached him in a break and asked him rather sharply what he was going to do in the scene. Ustinov replied that he thought he'd do almost nothing, at which Williams informed him that that would not be possible as he would be the one doing almost nothing. He could have worked in the City.

But the point is that, however you choose to express your attitude towards it, work determines the shape of our day, puts bread on our table and often charts the course of our entire life, sometimes curiously appearing to have a greater influence than family or friends. And when the Work Foundation asked people in 2004 if they were satisfied with their work, two-thirds said yes and only 15 per cent said no. That does mean about four million people hate their work – and there's probably a high chance of a close correlation between them and rude people – but the rest of us range from content to, if not ecstatic, at least a very reasonable level of enthusiasm about it.

But it always feels as if there is an outpouring of complaint and grumbling in the press and in con-versation about work and about the levels of service in Britain. So we are in danger of creating the impression that we are a nation of Victor Meldrews working ourselves up into a lather over the fact that every minute of our day our sensitivities are being trampled on, our faces metaphorically slapped and our noses put out of joint by slovenly colleagues, boorish bosses, arrogant managers, idiots on the phone, rude shop-keepers and general mistreatment at the hands of our fellow countrypeople. But as is so frequently the case with this whole subject, manners are more often than not only noticed in the breach. The minute somebody is rude to you, the lack of manners in Britain shoots up by a full 100 per cent. It hits us hard and personally. We don't like it and we extrapolate immediately.

But in fact at work most people make a considerable effort to be decent to each other and to customers. Is it worse than it was? It may only be, as ministers anxious not to sacrifice too many footie fan votes always say about the hooligans, the bad apples that spoil it for the rest of us. In shops they are the ones who sneer and raise their eyebrows in disbelief if we say we're a size twelve or have a thirty-inch waist. In the office, they are the ones who never bother to get to know you, cut you dead in the corridor, don't smile, never think of you and steal your ideas. Sometimes you think they're the kind of people Machiavelli would call devious. They're stealth sourpusses, gliding under the radar of the boss and aiming straight at you.

However, in general people do try and make work work for them and their colleagues. But manners are too often undercut by what else we're being told, which is to be ambitious, to strive and be goal-oriented. We are encouraged to clamber to the top of the pile and inevitably that can have casualties. You don't have to stand on the shoulders of minnows and trample on their hopes to get to the peak. But it can happen. And not only can simple ambition, perhaps only temporarily, shred our manners but people's desire to behave well to colleagues is also frequently undermined by the reality of the insecurity of our situation at work. Increasingly change is not just embraced in business but worshipped. And that can throw us all into undeniable competition with each other. There can be, particularly in the private sector, very real divisions between us at work. We all may be getting on famously, but we're also having to watch our backs. Then overlaid on that come the very best intentions of managers and the very best efforts of the human resources people. They understand that we want to get the best out of work and develop our potential to the full. However, that has lurched into the kind of hyperbole where apparently we 'thirst for empowerment', we 'hunger for delegation', we desire more than we can say to 'build bonds' with our 'team-mates'. We do want all of those things. But steady on. Saying that would be fine if there hadn't been an exponential increase in the bullshit factor which management training has generated over the last decade or so. It leaves us all gasping desperately for just some simple clarity in relationships with people who should be our bosses, but are now posing as our friends, and colleagues with whom we just work, but with whom sometimes it feels we're being encouraged to live in a community. At the moment these are good reasons for people to feel confused about how to behave towards colleagues at work as boundaries are shifting fast.

The notion of change has dominated the workplace of late. If you ever took Course 101 in basic capitalism at evening class you may remember Joseph Schumpeter, the economist who fled Austria from the Nazis and taught at Harvard for the rest of his life. Well, in his book *Capitalism, Socialism and Democracy* he used the concept of creative destruction to describe the way in which our Western economies could never be stationary. Change which drove growth was constant in capitalism, he thought. The trouble for us is that managers particularly are taking that literally. Schumpeter didn't approve of it; he merely noticed it. Managers, however, are embracing it. And the problem for the rest of us is that until quite recently our generations haven't really experienced it before. For a period after the Second World War in the advanced economies the combination of strong trades unions, the welfare state and the dominance of large corporations as places where most of us worked produced a deceptive stability, which came to a screeching halt in the late seventies. And what we are now experiencing is this constant change. And at work most people perceive it as a threat. A small number of people find it bracing, but to most it's very destabilising. Change is very unnerving, yet it's becoming a way of life. And it is making people very dispensable at work, not for reasons to do with their ability to do the job, but because their company has merged, or demerged, or gone public, or been part of an MBO, or been restructured, or re-engineered, or downsized, or upsized, or gone to the ladies' chamber. Sorry. But it's bewildering to people because this disrupts the narrative of their lives and they don't know where they stand with their employers. In one breath everybody is talking about teamwork and how all the staff are one big happy family. And in the next the company has dispensed with your services and has given you rather more opportunity to spend time with your own. The reasons why you may or may not continue to work where you have been is no longer based on clear-cut and definite rules, but on the ferocious demands of change. With competition being fierce, you are thus constantly pitted against your colleagues.

To a certain extent what used to help us steer our

way through this was a combination of formality which allowed you to understand exactly where you stood and trades unions which tried to protect you when you rebelled against it. Not in any way perfect, but at least you knew the score. Practically no one wants to go back there, but there may be an emerging desire for a degree of formality and structure at work again. Then, to be frank, you knew your place and you stuck to it. Unless you were Katharine Hepburn in *Woman of the Year* or *Adam's Rib*, by and large women typed and men managed. Of course, we love the fact that this has started to change. Manners need to encompass the shift. And also, as the number of people in heavy industry and manufacturing declines and brings with it the truth that, as the Work Foundation estimates, only one in five people in the private sector belong to a trades union, people are thrown back on their own resources for their protection. In the absence of collectively negotiated relationships with employees, managers need to give their staff absolute clarity in their relationship.

This kind of macro-economic talk is not a very great distance at all from manners at the water cooler. In an uneasy world employers recognise the need to drive their companies forward by engaging the ingenuity and creativity of the staff and the staff want to find some stability and ease with their workmates. So huge amounts of resources and thought are currently invested in getting workers to enjoy work, trust their colleagues and bond with each other. And the Work Foundation and the City & Guilds Happiness index and all the other bits of research tell us that if we feel valued and feel part of a joint enterprise, we are far more happy and far more productive at work. And thus probably far better mannered to each other. Yet at the same time as we are running up mountains or spending days in all-company samba drumming workshops, when the chips are down we are still out for ourselves in a very competitive environment. Manners and money, manners and ambition, manners and insecurity do not always sit terribly well together.

While this mustn't drift into melodrama, with Snow White's stepmother cackling in the background rubbing her hands in glee at the mirror, taken down a notch or two it does represent some of the truth that underlies our relationships at work. People can appear as sweet as pie but to some extent everyone is jockeying for position. So that's why people try and take credit for ideas that were actually not theirs. They try and cut other people out of the information loop. They talk people down in their absence. They suck up to the manager. In other words, they are very bad mannered. The difficulty is that business is there to achieve certain goals but one of them is not good manners. It is perfectly possible to go on a training course on how being polite to customers is good for business in a company where the culture inside is anything but one of politeness.

Alongside this runs the second destabilising force in people's work life – what we might call the manager as friend, chumanagement. Someone I know who runs a company that grew very fast about five years ago described the dilemma perfectly. When asked what the difference was in his life between starting the company and now running it as a plc, he said, 'I can't go to the pub after work with everybody any more. Because it makes managing people impossible.' David Brent's failure to understand this at Wernham Hogg in *The Office* is what has made Ricky Gervais such a toe-curling fortune. He wanted to be liked far too much. No one wants to be lashed to a machine like a slave or humiliated by a time-and-motion process, where pee breaks are measured to the last second, but equally no one really wants to be friends with the boss. The trouble is that in an increasingly informalised workplace, lots of bosses feel they have to be liked by their employees. So everybody has moved on to first-name terms, which feels a helluva lot more enjoyable than all the stuffed shirt calling of the boss Mr This or Mrs That. But blurred boundaries are more easily crossed. A most vivid example of this has been dress-down Fridays. Research by Dr Beverly Block in the School of Business Administration at Missouri Southern State University showed that, while they may have been intended to develop all sorts of matey matey bonding and *esprit de corps*, in fact absenteeism rose, people swore more, flirted more and the experiment generally gave rise to all sorts of behaviour that in turn gave the human resources wallahs heart attacks. Dress-down Fridays weren't a great success. Their demise may typify the fact that at work people are currently looking for a few more limits. Yet we also want more enjoyment.

It sometimes feels, with all the talk of work/life balance, that we're trying to go back to a bucolic sense of work where we were just hunter-gatherers working apparently for the simple pleasure of it. But simultaneously trying to combine that with an underlying yet rapacious desire to have a car, many white goods and several different kinds of bread in the bin. Marshall Sahlins, the great American anthropologist, has called the hunter-gatherers the original affluent society. But when he did, he was scoffed at by other academics, who were focusing on simple material poverty. However, if you take a more Zen view that human material wants and necessities are relatively few and that it might be worth working for reasons simply of health and happiness rather than to satisfy the fetish of material acquisition, then the hunter-gatherers were pretty well-off. They were lucky chaps who lived a kind of utopian existence well away from mobile phones, fax machines, Fat Controllers and spotty bosses who seem to make our lives a misery. And since the oldest complete hunting weapons, discovered in 1997 in Schöningen in Germany, date from about four hundred thousand years ago, it's not that unreasonable to assume that the hunter-gatherers led a moderately successful way of life. If you accept that cultural man has been on earth for about two million years, then for about 99 per cent of it he was a-hunting and a-gathering.

And just to give you a taste, if you read the work of the anthropologist Richard Lee, who spent time studying people living in the Kalahari, he discovered that when they didn't have a very successful time hunting they would just stop and go and spend time dancing with their neighbours. Can you imagine? The Hadza people of Tanzania have managed to get hunting down to two hours a day and prefer to spend the rest of the day gambling. The Yir-Yoront, Aborigines living on the Cape York Peninsula in northern Australia, intriguingly have a word for work, but it doesn't cover hunting. *Woq* means a variety of chores, but the occupation that is their main task of survival is not thought of as work.

You can make long lists of these kinds of examples, but, of course, it's a daft dream to think that we will even touch the hem of the loincloth of a hunter-gatherer in our search to enjoy work more. But there are signs that we are reacting against the increasing pressure that we feel at the moment. Almost a third of people in 2000 said, when asked by the Policy Studies Institute and the LSE, that work was preventing them carrying out their family duties. This was almost 10 per cent higher than eight years earlier. This is presumably why Datamonitor, the market analysts, are predicting that by 2007 more than three and a half million people will have what they rather inelegantly called 'downshifted'; in other words they will have traded a drop in income for a better quality of life spending more time with their families.

That's not an option available to all of us. But even if we don't have the chance to shift down, we still want to improve dramatically our experience of work. If we were clearer about manners, it might be a small contribution. So it's worth thinking about:

- How you behave with colleagues.
- How you deal with ambition.
- How you deal with customers.

COLLEAGUES – AND HOW TO BEHAVE WITH THEM

Let's just say from the top there are some basic manners at work. No matter your ontological insecurity in a globalised world, the undermining of your feelings of wellbeing by the threat of potential downsizing, or the difficulty of handling the competition with your colleagues, for goodness sake open the door. And smile at people in the corridor and ask how people in the office are. Just don't be a grouch. The weather is bad enough in Britain without having a small thunderstorm in the corner of the room all day. Make work bearable. You don't have to smile like a maniac; just acknowledge that other people exist. There's something human going on here.

Now it's entirely possible that those with mean minds will think that if you say, hi to the boss when you pass her in the corridor you are sucking up. Well, if you hide behind the photocopier for hours on the off chance that she'll wander by and you can leap out and smile, then you're a sap and deserve the suspicion of colleagues. But hello or hi should know few boundaries of status.

Likewise, any boss who ignores a well-meant hello shouldn't be out and about because they obviously can't cope with human beings. When he was director of the National Theatre, Richard Eyre told me once that he used to try and get to his office by a different route through the backstage as often as possible so that he had the chance to bump into different staff on the way through. But he wasn't foolish enough to think that he was making friends with them; he was just being visible. If you are the boss, do try and remember you are not their friend. If anyone ever thinks about what they want in an employer, they always reach the same conclusion fairness and certainty. Lots of different employers and managers do it in different ways, usually as a factor of their personality, but the successful ones offer clarity. Some bosses are loud, demanding and infuriating, others modest and quiet. At a farewell drink I went to once the person leaving thanked their boss for showing them how to deal with people. A pause. And how not to. The laughter in the room was affectionate. For all his mad enthusiasm this boss gave his employees leadership and they just understood and put up with his eccentricities. Manners at work are not the mechanical application of principle. They are a negotiation between the non-human demands of business and organisations – the demands of the bottom line – and the desire we have to get along with each other.

At a conference, organised by the Common

Purpose network in 2004, of people who chair boards of both public and private organisations, we were asked to name two regrets. A significant number of people identified one of them as an occasion where they hadn't had the sense of purpose swiftly to get rid of a senior manager who they knew was damaging the organisation. It is not always easy to be single-minded about that responsibility. It can be scary to sack people. It's easier to avoid it, to find a way round it, to procrastinate. But if you have muddied the waters with chummy chummy chat instead of paying your staff the respect of treating them honestly, it's even more difficult to reward and promote them sincerely or to lay them off cleanly and fairly. The formality of the agreed procedures is what will make the, frankly not overpleasant, process a lot easier for both sides.

Between colleagues, rather than boss and staff, the greatest difficulty about being nice to people at work is that you may not actually like them. You may not hate them, but you just don't choose them as your friends. You may have nothing in common with them, find them plain dull or politically disagreeable. None of which, however, stops you working with them. It just stops you liking them. There are two types. The first category is people who you just think are lousy at their job. You have no respect for their talent; in fact, you're in awe of their lack of it. And you resent the fact that you have to carry them. These people you have to complain about. Well, that's what it says in management textbooks. And, yeah, sure, you're going to do that when it's a minefield of politics, gossip and competition. The best you can do in this situation is to find out what other people think, because if everybody thinks they're a deadbeat, then you can try and do something about it. But be careful. Be sure that your own motives can be seen as transparent. People will take any opportunity to call you a sneak, if you're not careful. Good manners probably dictate that, difficult as it may be, you try and tell them first what you think of them. But the purpose of that would have to be to try and get them to improve, not merely to be rude to them. Without any reference to your own skills or ability, give them specific examples of what is bugging you about what they're doing – or not doing. On no account compare them with yourself or anybody else. The minute you do that it will all spin out of control as they then attack the others, or you, rather then look at their own behaviour. The point of manners is to give limits to enable you to handle the conversation. Manners should help you to contain it, not help you to be nice to them.

The second group are pretty much impossible to deal with without getting pretty close to being rude. Their very presence takes you back to school. They are the office bore, the person who always wants to come to the pub. They are the one who no one likes, the last one to be chosen for the soccer or the netball team. They hang around you like a torn piece of loo paper does to the sole of your shoe. It's agony to write this down because it involves thinking of them lurking expectantly waiting to be included, desperate to be wanted. Every time my friend Pete leaves his office at the end of the day, his version of this character is fiddling with the lock on their office door waiting to chat and be asked to the pub. Writing this down is giving me eczema. And what most people want to do in this situation is to whisper behind their backs and make sure they don't discover which pub it is.

However you deal with it, what this situation questions is the line between friendship and work. Manners do not dictate that you have to be friends with people at work. Manners are not just about bringing people closer; they're about managing hostility and difference. Friendship at work is dangerous because it crosses all boundaries of the functional relationships we have with each other there. You know perfectly well if you're becoming a real friend with someone and manners dictate that if that happens, you draw a clear line between your relationship at work and your friendship. And to those with whom we don't actually want to be friends, we learn to lie. Not seriously but for the sake of preserving the balance between the closeness we need to work together and the distance we need not to be friends. And that's fine. A couple of examples.

'We must have lunch' means we never will, but I want you to know that we still might be useful to each other. Let's meet doesn't mean let's meet. It only means let's meet if you are actually working together and need to. Let's meet is a way of keeping the option open. Don't get out your diary. Put off fixing the exact time and date until later. In fact, it's useful never to have your diary with you as that way you can never commit and can always reserve your options. Good manners? Well, it's worse manners to cross boundaries of intimacy when there is no basis for it.

Which leads us to the issue of office romance. Flirting, and more, with each other is going great guns at work right now. In July 2002 Fish4jobs polled nine thousand people and concluded that 25 per cent of us meet our partners at work. And in *Sex and Business*, Shere Hite, the woman who knocked the stuffing out of the boasts about the male orgasm, found that 62 per cent of women and 71 per cent of men have had an affair with a colleague. (And does the 9 per cent difference mean that they're either gay or they've had more than one affair? We'll never know.) The last chapter in this book gives relationships and manners the complete rub down. But, for the purposes of this chapter, at work it poses really only one problem. But size does matter in this case because it's a huge one. Romance, or at least to be blunt, sex, and work is beset with the problem of permission.

If A and B's eyes lock across the photocopier or during Any Other Business they are thinking of exactly that and bells ring and you hear the pitter-patter of tiny feet as everybody runs to the canteen to gossip about how Mandy and Dave, or Robert and Mark, or Sarah and Julia have fallen madly in love, then the problem is minimal. Even if it's a slower burn, but entirely mutual, all you have to make certain is that as soon as you are sure you tell your boss and continue to treat each other as colleagues rather than snookums and sneekums. If manners are about the clarity of relationships at work then if you're sharing a bed don't start to share a desk or, worse, coochie-coo looks across meetings.

The time when things spiral towards nastiness, of course, is when unwanted advances are the currency of one person's desire. In a public space where you meet by accident you can tell them to F-off if they pinch your bum or make lewd suggestions. Or if that's not your style, then be as subtle as you like. And just leave. There seems to be no requirement for polite-ness to someone who has trespassed on your body or your sensitivities. However, it's substantially more difficult when you are locked in daily contact with them at work. Manners previously might, in some strange perversion of chivalrous logic, have required unwanted sexual remarks, however apparently innocent, to be taken as compliments. And women underwent untold humiliations. Without her glasses Miss Jones may have been beautiful but now without her glass ceiling she is rightly a lot more powerful. As are gay men and women, who also suffer from the unwanted attention of predators. Add to that the racism still suffered by too many people in the work place and the question you want to ask is, in whatever form it takes, when is it good manners to point out someone's gender, race or sexuality? Because whether the harassment is sexual, homophobic or racist it flows from the fact that you are no longer treating that person properly, which would be as a colleague to be valued on their talents at work. So when is it polite to point out difference?

There is a balance and, notwithstanding the obvious examples of harassment, it's not always easy to get it right. Chairing a disability conference last year, I was trying to put it scrupulously into practice and be studiedly neutral and direct. So, in a most extreme and, I stress, fictional example, if there had been a lesbian in an iron lung in the third row I was determined to call her to speak by simply saying 'the woman in pink'. Now you may think I was being frantically overcautious but that's how David Dimbleby deals with it at *Question Time*, and I thought I would take my lead from him. There is no need to make any reference to people's disability. Then, about halfway through a plenary session, a man in a blue shirt put his hand up. So I said, 'the man in the blue shirt'. Nothing happened. I said again, 'the man in the blue shirt. You there, in the middle.' Since he had his hand up and no one else was speaking he then realised it must be him I was talking about. A slightly mischievous grin spread across his face as he said, 'Look, man, how do I know if I've got a blue shirt on. I'm blind.' The path to hell etc. . . .

Manners used to require a rigid separation between personal life and work life. The sangfroid of the Englishman and the stiff upper lip and all that. Doncha know? But when personal politics became one of the drivers of social change, work became one of its main arenas. With the Equal Pay Act in 1970 and the Race Relations Act in 1976, the state put under seal in Gothic calligraphy the people who were to be protected at work. Since then have been added disabled people, gay people and the old. In legislation it's rude not to mention them. In fact it's entirely necessary to do so. But in conversation and relationships at work it may not be. Already you can feel those concerned wanting to move beyond being noticed. They want to be recognised for what they can do, not who they are. Until, of course, someone tries to limit what they can do because of who they are. And then they need it noticed a lot by way of protection. But while politics may require that in order to right imbalances and rebalance wrongs, we name and claim protection for certain groups of people, manners require that we treat people with respect and neutrality at work as colleagues. Manners are there to manage difference, not to create social change.

While we are rightly concerned with notions of including people in relation to equalities and rights at work, we have to stop doing it with e-mail. This is getting silly. E-mail is not an alternative form of fly posting. E-mail has turned into a combination of a small child constantly tapping on the back of your knee. And litter. People grumble that the art of letter writing is dead. Well, the art of litter writing certainly isn't. E-mails are alive and well and driving us all barmy. If we go back to one of the underlying principles of this chapter, I have been arguing that a degree of honesty about our relationships at work can guide our manners. The desire to cc the entire world into every communication is too often rather a huge exercise in arse-covering masquerading as the appearance of inclusivity. What I mean by that is that the electronic medium has allowed us to send everything to everybody, which creates the illusion that communication has actually happened and that information has passed. But, of course, because opening your inbox now is like opening your front door and your dustman emptying your bin into the hall, no one reads half of what is sent to them. This is not sincerely meant communication between human beings. Either they are mails needlessly copying you in on things you never needed or wanted to know in the first place, or more that half of them require just the merest click in order to give us the warmish feeling that we have helped find a child orphaned by the Asian tsunami, made an impact on world poverty or freed a political prisoner in Myanmar, to name just three that have come my way in the last twenty-four hours. Is e-mail driving us to treat each other with a terrible lack of manners?

Is it actually good manners to cc the entire world on every bit of correspondence? On one level e-mail feels a surprisingly personal medium as it comes to us directly on to our own little computer. And if there is any level of discrimination about who is on the list of recipients then it does a certain amount to bind together a group of people in a common cause around a joint project. As we saw with funerals, it can be a way of easily and without show or fuss creating warmth and a network of support in moments of great grief. E-mail, its speed and the shape of it (if we can so call the formality of the subject field and the cc) gives us a way of knowing that we belong to a group. Used indiscriminately, though, it is just junk mail by a trendier name. Whether it's an unsolicited ad for Viagra (which, frankly, runs the risk of being received as a bit of an insult in any case) or a sloppy circulation of a company memo via a scattergun transgresses the need for manners to be born of conscious decision. If we want e-mail to be well mannered, in other words to bind us together through communication, we have to be careful, literally, about how we handle it and not allow its perfect electronic ease to become a one-click lack of thoughtfulness.

The conventions, therefore, have to be ones of consideration. And knowing that there are people who will recycle anything, even though not for environmental reasons, we have to remember that any e-mail must be assumed not to be private. Those wishing to be well-mannered and self-conscious with their use of e-mail are thus careful to be discreet. Others are not. We all probably remember with something of a shudder in 2000 the awful rudeness done to a woman in a City law firm who sent an explicitly racy, detailed but personal recollection of the night they'd spent together to a man who then forwarded it on to his mates. Within hours it had been circulated, according to *ComputerWeekly.com*, to over ten million people. The man and five of his colleagues were, according to the same magazine, disciplined by their employer. In another slightly lighter case, ten staff were sacked and eighty suspended by insurance company Royal & Sun Alliance for circulating an e-mail containing graphics of Kermit the Frog and Bart Simpson having sex.

The woman in question in the incident mentioned above (and to name her here would simply be to compound the wrong) had her private correspondence transformed by a process of malign electronic alchemy and unpleasant male boasting into a global whirlpool of prurient press interest. E-mail tempts us into casual actions. And because manners are self-conscious and not accidental, it might also lead us to wonder about whether there is any meaningful purpose to our actions when our compassion is detonated merely by the click of a mouse. Manners would suggest that we don't allow the facility of e-mail to shorthand the bonds between us, whether that's between strangers on the other side of the world or colleagues at the other end of the room.

That probably means starting e-mails to people you do not know well with Dear whoever and ending them with your name. If you want people to feel that you have thought about what you are saying to them seriously, you might like to check spelling and punctuation, not because of some prissy head teacher who's going to keep you in detention if you don't, but because communication that appears to be more thoughtful than less has a stronger chance of cementing bonds between us. And if we are helped to keep clear boundaries between us at work then formality will emphasise that. Although, in contrast, of course, e-mails between friends, as we have found with the discussion of manners throughout this book, follow entirely different rules based on the dynamics of closeness and trust rather than distance.

AMBITION – THE TENSIONS OF TEAMWORK AND THE ILLUSION OF GOBBELDEGOOK

We are anxious about the expression of ambition. And we still don't know whether it's good or bad manners to talk about money. In the film *Wall Street* Gordon Gekko said, 'Greed is good'. But in Britain, while boasting about the country is pretty standard – you will have noticed that any politician worth his or her salt will always claim that we have the best army/police/actors/probably even traffic wardens in the world – personal boasting is generally frowned on. Of course, there's plenty of greed here, it's just that it's been better not to talk about it. There's always been a kind of morbid discretion required around wealth in Britain. Until that is, the eighties appeared, the decade that thought it was Alexis Carrington. A culture was ushered in, in which Harry Enfield could invent Loadsamoney brandishing his wad of cash from his back pocket, but which immediately turned the satire into national adulation. Across classes, wealth was shoulder-padded to people. Ostentation was the new black, poverty the ultimate unfashionable accessory. People were proud to preen. But these things go in waves. I am sure Midas was a notoriously big tipper but Bill Gates, despite his immense riches, is seldom seen dressed in anything other than chinos. He affects a kind of modesty in lifestyle. Despite being the richest man alive, he still tries to look like a geek. And his inevitably ruthless success in business is masked under the soft image of philanthropy. Perhaps Gates has read Erasmus: 'the greater a man's wealth, the more agreeable is his modesty. To those of lesser means one should allow the consolation of modest self-pride.'

The nineties retreated into stealth wealth. People weren't any less rich. In fact, the rich got richer. The gap between rich and poor, the Work Foundation estimated in *The Joy of Work*, widened so that between 1979 and 2004 they went from being 2.9 times as rich as the poor to four times. But still executives wore GAP. As these fads twist and turn, it's dizzyingly difficult to keep up with the mood swings of politeness. What are the manners of wealth? Is it rude to ask what people earn? Is it ruder to tell them?

John McGrath, the political actor and writer, founded a theatre company in Scotland, which he named 7:84 in an attempt to draw attention to the statistic at the time that 7 per cent of the world owned 84 per cent of the wealth. The company was a success and John, sadly now dead, became a notable writer for stage and TV. He managed eventually to indulge himself a tiny bit and buy a Range Rover. On the back he put the company sticker: 7:84. One day in a petrol station, the man at the pump asked him what it stood for. He patiently explained that 7 per cent of the world owned 84 per cent of the wealth. And the pump attendant looked at the Range Rover and said, 'That's all very well, pal, but there's no need to brag about it.'

One of the most surprising findings of *The Joy of Work* report was that ambition and money are important to only about half the British workforce. Most people are happy with their salaries and startlingly undemanding about their levels of job satisfaction. Most people work to live and are happy to do so at their current level. So at work ambitious people, while admired, a fact testified to by the constant choice of Richard Branson as a role model by young people in newspaper polls, are also treated with certain wariness. How you handle ambition at work may be not so much a matter of manners as of tactics. Showing your boss that you want his job may be foolish. Showing his boss that you want your boss's job may be a clever move. We are pitted against each other and manners may only help to manage that conflict. But they will probably involve a level of dishonesty. Why should you not open the door, smile at people in the corridor and ask how people are, just because you have your eye on their job or a desire to do better than them? Yet people will accuse you of being two-faced. But would it make the work environment worse if you treated them badly and did none of those things? Of course it would. What you have to do is to be as clear and open about the conflict when you can and decent and polite in all your dealings with them.

I have been arguing and restating the case for honesty at least in the recognition of the underlying conflicts for people at work because there has grown up a culture of linguistic befuddlement in the way people are attempting to communicate with one another at work. I was sent a document the other day which contained the immortal piece of information that 'the floor targets were flowing from the problem trees'. How poetic. I have absolutely no idea what that means. We are drowning in 'strategic added value' and 'prioritised agendas'. It feels like a giant April Fool's Day prank. Recently I told a government official, as a joke, that the development on the allotments at the back of where I live meant that the council were engaging in a 'staggered process of de-allotmentisation'. You may not believe me, but it's true, if I tell you that the phrase has now appeared in an official document. The twisted tongue of gobble-degook is pretending to organise our working lives. People are speaking a language which, it is hardly surprising to discover, obscures the reality of relation-ships. We need to fight back. If I am right and manners need clarity to manage the difficulty and possible hostility between us at work, then let me provide you with a guide to how not to speak to each other at work, by way of a warning. And if someone memo-ises the problem trees at you, use the generator below to toss them back a reply.

It is a bullshit generator. To use it, think of a three-digit number anywhere between 000 and 999. The first digit refers to a word in column A, the second digit to a word in column B and the third to a word in column C.

Column A	Column B	Column C
1 integrated	1 management	1 options
2 definitive	2 organisational	2 parameters
3 responsive	3 real-time	3 capability
4 optimised	4 reciprocal	4 payback
5 effective	5 digital	5 programming
6 deductive	6 logic	6 concepts
7 proactive	7 strategic	7 framework
8 customised	8 incremental	8 projections
9 task-led	9 systems	9 objectives
0 ongoing	0 sustainable	0 contingency

You may combine the three columns in any way to produce, say, 176 'integrated strategic concepts' and 733 'proactive real-time capability'. Endless fun for all the family and a shot across the bows of those who would stir up sludge in the clear waters of our communications with one another.

And, finally, a word or two about the manners of dealing with customers in person and on the phone.

CUSTOMERS – HOW CALL CENTRES AND SHOPS COULD DO BETTER

Call centres and shops are hotbeds of poor manners, not, in the main, because people are just gratuitously rude but because they are set an impossible task and not given the training or scope to use their own initiative. Cold-calling from call centres is reaching epidemic proportions. About half a million people work in call centres in the UK and about two-thirds of them rang me last Thursday. You know it's them. They are the ones who ring and ask for Mr Farshave. Simeon Fornshaw. Yet at the same time as getting my name wrong they are committing the first offence of bad manners by lurching straight into an uninvited intimacy. And they always tell us they're not selling anything. So you wonder why they are ringing. If everybody just put the phone down we could kill the market. But there must be some of you who are taking these calls and, worse, some of you who are actually buying things. This is not working for either side. The call centre staff don't really want to be there. They have to earn a living but if they had a choice would they be ringing people they don't know, trying to sell them things they'd never heard of, for prices they can hardly believe? No. And you don't want them ringing you either. So let's all call a truce. Politely, next time they ring, put the telephone down. They're used to people slamming it down, but it's humiliating enough to be working in a call centre without suffering constant rejection with added rudeness. So be gentle and let them go.

Then there are the call centres that we have to ring. We know that most call centre work is dismal. We know that 68 per cent of you are women, almost half of you are part-time and that you only earn about £12,000 a year. But still the sheer lack of manners in the whole exercise is staggering. On both sides. And it flows directly from the fact that no manager in any call centre anywhere in the world ever trained any telephonist to take a decision. So both sides of the conversation treat each other appallingly. Frustrated customers shout and get stroppy and the telephonist is barely able to help because, as Basil used to say about Manuel in *Fawlty Towers*, they 'know nothing'. Or if they do, more importantly no one has given them the latitude or the training to do anything about it. So you end up with an exchange like the one that follows. It happened to me and it's fairly typical.

I bought a new telephone recently. Well, it's more than a phone. It's a diary, an address book, it can e-mail, it can text and, if I could work out which command to give it, it can probably make pizza. To be quite honest, if it could hold its own in an intelligent discussion about Almodóvar, who would ever need to look for a lover? This thing knows more about my life than I do. It remembers names of people that I have forgotten I ever met. When I put a change of address into the contacts list you can feel it thinking 'they've traded up'. Anyway, it went wrong shortly after I got it. Not terribly wrong, just a glitch. I had looked in the handbook and couldn't work out what to do, so I rang the call centre where the immediate lack of human contact cast me into Manners Hell.

After pushing 'one' for technical support, 'one' again for the kind of gizmo that I wanted to ask about and 'two' to be put in a long queue before being patronised for a quarter of an hour by someone who knows even less than me, I got through to Helen. Perfectly sweet. I am sure she's a great mother. I told her what the problem was and she said she was 'going to run a diagnostic'. I asked her what that meant. There was a pause. She said it meant that she was 'going to run a diagnostic'. Although she said the words with a slightly different emphasis, hoping to fool me into thinking that she was saying something different. You could feel her raise an eyebrow and look knowingly at one of her colleagues: 'I've got a guy here who doesn't know what running a diagnostic means.' I now felt like an Englishman trying to make myself understood in Paris, where eyebrows are permanently formed into an Arc de Triomphe of superiority. So I waited while Helen did her thing. Her thing turned out to be to read out to me the exact words on the exact same page of the handbook that I had in front of me. I said, 'You're reading from the handbook.' She said, 'I am running a diagnostic.' I said, 'What's running . . .?' No, I didn't. But she said, 'Don't be rude, sir, or I'll put the phone down.' I said 'Look, I don't want to be rude. But why don't I speak directly to technical support?' 'Sorry, sir, but we can't put you straight through to technical support.' 'Why not?' 'They're busy.' 'Who with?' 'I can't tell you that, sir.' The 'sir' was beginning to grate now. 'But if you can't put anyone through to them, then who are they talking to?' She said, 'If you're going to be rude, sir.' I know, you're going to put the phone down. 'Look,' I said, 'I don't want you to take offence at this' – and at this point I knew I was jousting with the possibility of maximum retaliation and hostility – 'but to be honest, Helen, you don't know anything more about this than I do. This is the blind leading the blind. Why don't I just talk to technical support? '

So she put the phone down.

Her lack of training just became rudeness. No one was allowing her to use her intelligence. People ought to be encouraged to be quick-witted and to use their natural charm and initiative to enjoy solving problems. If we want manners in customer service people need to be trained and encouraged to do that. It could be so different. I heard a story once and I don't care if it's true. It makes the point. There was a young lad who worked in a supermarket in London. He was asked by a customer for half a head of lettuce. He said to the man, 'We don't do half a head of lettuce.' 'Well,' said the man, 'I'd like half a head of lettuce. So could you go and find the supervisor and ask him if I can have one.' So the boy sloped off to the storeroom, where he said to the manager, 'Some dickhead out there says he wants half a head of lettuce.' And as he said it he suddenly noticed that the man was standing right behind him. So he added, 'And this nice gentleman wants the other half.' Later the manager said to the boy, 'Now that's the kind of quick-wittedness we want to see more of in this company. Where do you come from?' 'Manchester,' said the boy. 'Why did you leave?' ''cos it's full of footballers and whores,' said the boy. 'Oh really?' said the manager. 'My wife comes from Manchester.' Quick as a flash the boy replied, 'What team does she play for?'

All right, so it's a joke. But you get the point. Initiative makes manners. And with call centres and customer service generally there's a bit of effort to be made on both sides. Managers need to help their staff.

How can people ever be helpful if you won't let them? If all they do all day is parrot procedure, run diagnostics, tell you that what they've got, is what's on the shelves then we are all on a hiding to frustration. But even if you work in a call centre and you feel that on some level you are doing something vaguely worthwhile – if only solving a tiny phone problem – then your working day might feel just a smidgeon more fulfilling. So if staff are trained to do what actually needs to be done to help, rather than just blindly following some procedure, then manners might improve.

And if you work in a shop, do try not to patronise us when we ask a question. We may appear stupid. That's because if we're asking you a question we are at that moment what sociologists call knowledge-deprived. In other words, right here and now, we are stupid. But please don't remind us, just help us. It's manners and the management of possible hostility again.

Of course, there are people who really are a bit dense. The British Tourist Authority in New York used to keep a book in which they wrote down the silliest questions they were asked. One man rang in and inquired whether you got a different view of the English countryside from the first class seats on the train than you did from the second. And Brits can be as daft. My mate who works in a bookshop, and who coined the phrase 'bitch button' to describe that which you barely need to press to produce a make-up-cracking explosion of rudeness from the most difficult customers, said that several people recently have asked for books by Harry Potter. And they will not accept the explanation that they are by J. K. Rowling. One woman just wouldn't stop insisting, 'Those are not what I want. I know about those. I want the ones by him, not about him.' This woman had her nose so far in the air towards a shop assistant it poked through a gap in the ozone layer.

There are bags of room in the retail relationship for hostility. It's pregnant with possibilities of war. Customers frequently treat shop staff with contempt as if they are servants unquestioningly obligated by their every request. Shop assistants talk to other staff or on mobiles as they supposedly serve us. Manners are designed to reduce the potential for anger in such situations. The relationship between customer and shop assistants and waiters and bar staff and all the rest of the people who work in the service industries are fantasies. Unless you're a regular, you'll never see each other again. For the brief time span of the transaction you're pretending that you're friends. So – and at this point give a little Jewish shrug and hit the word 'hurt' with special care – would it hurt you to pretend a little? It'll make for a nicer day.

And by the same token if you're a customer, do the assistant the favour of remembering that they, and call centre operatives and all the rest of them, probably don't love the job. They may make the best of it and have fun. And if they have a decent boss and decent colleagues they may actually enjoy being at work for most of the time. But they're not volunteering to save children. So, when you're a customer, try not to be the one whose behaviour makes it your soup they want to wee in. And if you're the shop assistant, do us all a favour and pretend that you want to help. Make the effort, everybody. See if it hurts.

The people on the stiff end of this relationship are the ones who live in the world of tips.

TIPPING

Tipping is a mystery to most of us. We do it. By and large we don't even mind doing it. But we have little or no idea why we do it. It's like those moments when you've gone into the kitchen and then realise you've no idea what for. If we thought tipping improved service, which is the most common assumption about why we do it, we'd tip everybody who served us. But we don't. On aeroplanes we never tip stewards yet lots of people tip taxi drivers even though there is precious little they can do to improve the service. They can take you the wrong way or they can crash, I suppose, but it's basically a case of 'please take me to X'. And, with or without an A–Z, they do. They could help you with your luggage, but next time that happens look up and see the pigs flying by. By tipping a taxi driver, it would seem that we are doing little more than following convention and giving in to social pressure.

Once I didn't tip a cabbie in New York because I asked to go to an address in TriBeCa, which is in the bottom of Manhattan and so outside the numerical grid. He was confused by the streets having names rather than numbers. So he got lost. So I reckoned he'd already spent the tip on the extra streets we'd gone up and down. And up and down again. So I didn't tip him. So he tried to reverse into me. So I jumped out of the way. So he hit the car behind. So I felt good.

Boswell reported that Dr Johnson jotted down in 1737, 'I had a cut of meat for sixpence and bread for a penny, and gave the waiter a penny; so that I was quite well served – nay, better than the rest, for they gave the waiter nothing.' And like Dr Johnson, we imagine tipping improves service. However – and this might be a bit obvious, but bear with me – service only improves where it can be improved. And secondly, if we thought it made the service better, wouldn't we always tip when we thought it might improve it? But as we've said above, we follow neither of these rules. If we did we'd only tip in bad restaurants, in the hope of improving the service. Also, we tip taxi drivers even though the service is not really open to improvement. So why do we tip and when did it start?

There are many theories about its origins, and many about why tips are called tips. Mark Brenner in *Tipping for Success*, in common with several others, says that it is an acronym of 'to insure promptitude'. This sounds plausible until you realise that it should be 'ensure', shouldn't it? Which would make it a tep. Which is as far removed from a tip as a tup is. And a tup is a ram. And what would a waiter want with one of those? And secondly, while tipping was common certainly by the sixteenth century, acronyms were not in use much before the 1920s. The most plausible source is probably the Romany word tip, which means to give. The *OED* defines 'tip' as 'rogues' cant' or 'medieval street talk' for 'give me your money'.

But why did the first tippers start giving money away? By definition they couldn't be conforming to any social norm. They were probably just being generous. In a research paper called 'Tipping: The Economics of a Social Norm', Ofer H. Azar says that in sixteenth-century England house guests started to tip the servants just for being extra helpful to them.

And by the end of the eighteenth century throughout Europe commercial tipping had become common. Curiously, in these days where tipping in the States is almost a thrice-hourly occurrence, American travellers used to home from Europe about how odd it was that people tipped there. There was no tipping in America until after the Civil War, which, of course, is logical. There was no servant class until after the Civil War, only slaves. Now in the States it is an epidemic. Ozer estimates the total tips in 2003 in restaurants alone was around $26 billion. That is more than the GNP of Albania, Ghana or Zaire and it's slightly less than Paraguay and Trinidad & Tobago added together, according to the figures from the geocities world information page

Although despite its prevalence in America now, in 1899 the *New York Times* claimed that the tipping practice was 'a wretched system that was originated and perpetuated not by its victims, the men who give and take tips, but by those who profit by it every year to the extent of millions more than a few. The real takers of tips are the hotel and restaurant proprietors . . . every tip saves the payment of wages to an equal amount . . .' Three years earlier *Gunton's Magazine* called tipping 'offensively un-American, because it was contrary to the spirit of American life of working for wages rather than fawning for favours'. Both publications openly campaigned against it.

Essentially, the three reasons for tipping are social convention, to depress wages or to reward good service. And no one has ever really objected to the last. Secretly I think we all imagine that these poorly paid waiters and porters live in tiny Dickensian garrets – or in a shoe with hundreds of children – and are dragging themselves through university with no money and only an aptitude for conceptual art or the sociology of the oxbow lake to make their way in the world. They are geniuses in the making or single mothers who are one step away from begging. So guilt plays out as generosity and we tip them.

Tipping has now become a habit, so we might usefully return it to a principle where service is rewarded, where tips are not automatic and where they are given with respect. Who, then, should we tip and how much?

Waiters

Ten to 15 per cent but absolutely depending on the service. Two things, though, are very important. Firstly, be nice to them. No one ever got spit in their cabbage by being a decent customer. And, secondly, check on whether the waiters themselves get the money. Too many managements nowadays are taking the tips. There's no particular problem with the tips being pooled so the bus boy, the waiter and the kitchen staff all get a cut; they've all contributed to your meal. But always check if the money you want to give goes directly to the staff. If it doesn't, the management are just adding to the cost of your meal indirectly. In New York in 1908 most of the porters in the top hotels went on strike because all the tips had to be passed to the head porter. The strike was successful. So at the very least in memory of the poor guys humping pigskin luggage for the overpampered in the early twentieth century, tip directly. Give tips in cash straight to the waiter or waitress. And don't do it surreptitiously as if you're passing 'my friend fancies you' or 'Miss Barnett is a lesbian' notes under the desk at school. Be up front and generous about it. If they've given you a good time, then a fair, open reward for service is quite the right thing.

Taxi drivers

Taxi drivers are mostly decent sorts and are appreciative if you do tip, but they shouldn't expect it. I still feel bad not tipping. But stiffen your spine. If they want to put up fares then they should. But why should we volunteer for a price hike? The only exception might be when they help with the luggage, shopping, pushchair or whatever.

Hairdressers

Again no need. They are charging a market price. You might want to show encouragement to any juniors hanging around, though, because they are usually on abysmal wages.

Of course, if you go regularly, stiffing might result in future revenge. Do you want to look like Peter Noone from Herman's Hermits for several weeks? On the other hand if they're going to cut your hair like the council, they'll only get the one chance because you're not going to go back. On balance, no need to tip. They should put their prices up if they want more money.

Porters, valet parking

Generally, tipping just seems to encourage employers to pay badly. But then not tipping seems just to encourage people to starve. So in the end I tip. But reluctantly.

Servants in country houses

Stop. You're fantasising now.

If you do ever end up in this situation, though, remember a story told by George Melly. He claims that a man he knew, who liked his drink, once stayed in a grand country house in Ireland. Never mind how drunk he got he always managed, before passing out, to lay out his notes and change on the small, low table in his room. One night he got up and went for a pee. Unfortunately on the small, low table in his room. The next morning the butler woke him with his breakfast. When the man finally got up to dress, he discovered that the butler had taken the still rather damp bank notes away and ironed them. Now that deserves a tip.

—m—

RELATIONSHIPS

The most famous Arab authority on love was a theologian, jurist and writer at the turn of the first millennium known as Ibn Hazm. And you'll understand why he had a nickname when you discover that his full name was Abu Muhammad Ali ibn Ahmad ibn Sa'id Ibn Hazm. I think that's all the Ibns. You can bet he was about half a mile away by the time his mother finished calling him in from the kasbah for his tea. He said, 'Of love the first part is jesting and the last part right earnestness.' And he was right. It starts in glorious jesting. It begins with a glance, a dance, a chance remark. Giddiness over-whelms us as we find wit and fun beyond our wildest dreams. Or so we feel. And then it continues in great earnestness. When it's good it changes the course of our lives. Either we bathe in years of ardent, nourishing love or it all ends in the zealousness of the battle of divorce or separation. I mean, there are the damp squibs that never really explode, chance encounters that promised the earth but turned out to be married (dull), recovering from a relationship (even duller) or who just gave you their phone number with one digit wrong (cunning). The promise of love can be devastatingly unfulfilled.

But false starts excepted – setting aside the moments when you thought it was the real thing but hours, days later, you discovered that it wasn't – love never just drifts away. It leaves rudely, abruptly, without apology, devastating you in its wake; or it can and often does, in an alchemic reverse, turn from gold to base metal through duty and routine. As feminists used to warn of relationships with men when I was a student, it starts when you sink into his arms and it ends with your arms in the sink. With precocious wisdom, that was scrawled on the loo door in the university library along with 'My mother made me a homosexual'. Underneath: 'If I send her the wool, will she make me one too?' And 'Free Nelson Mandela'. The triple gospels of realism, wit and hope. And if romance ever ignites at all, its begins with you idolising each other but it can still end, as Woody Allen once remarked of his wife, when you put them underneath a pedestal. And that's the case whether you're gay, straight, bi, happy with a little furry animal or just desperately and serially unsuccessfully seeking Susan or Shaun for the last twenty years.

So if you too feel a certain reluctance about this chapter, I don't blame you. It may well be because you too know that it is almost impossible to treat the subject of manners and romance and relationships as if there is a set of rules that can be deduced, written down and, even more unlikely, obeyed. Because there are no guarantees. Certainly not that if you behave in a certain way it'll promise a certain outcome. But worse than that, when you're in the grip of love, you have no control over your behaviour at all. So you can't even promise to behave properly. You hurt people despite your best intentions. You are disappointed despite your highest hopes. And you pursue people in the most hopeless situations against your better judgement. You never meant to end up without shoes at three in the morning, sobbing at their window till they called the police, who then got the benefit of a whole set more of your views on the person in question. But you did. Love drove you to it. Encouraged by drink. And how you behaved certainly can't be rationalised as even approaching good manners.

And in case you are in the least bit curious. No. Not me. A great friend.

Certainly, if you're a boy you can pursue romance with, if not complete bad faith, a certain single-minded myopia driven by very little else but desire. You can even be physically attracted while intellectually you know that any relationship, of even the briefest kind in or out of doors, with the person in question would be a complete disaster. You desire them but you know that you're driving towards self-destruction. It's almost definitely the same for women. It's just that women have a reputation for being marginally more sensible about it. But only marginally. Men know when they are overwhelmed by romance and helpless to control their behaviour. The comedian John Dowie once mordantly remarked that he saw his future wife in a club. Their eyes met across a smoke-filled dance floor and he thought to himself that that was the woman who was going to divorce him in five years time.

If manners can help around romance and love it's only because there is such possibility for hurt, such insecurity and uncertainty that they can smoothe the unevenness of the path by offering a little predictability. They can't guarantee the outcome, but they can make the process a little less harsh. Nothing softens rejection or hurt, but over the centuries manners have attempted to give form to the pursuit of desire.

So we could all agree without much contradiction that in seeing, asking, dating, loving and living with someone there are perhaps just three basic rules. Don't ever hurt them physically or emotionally. Always be faithful to them. And never leave the loo seat up. The last you can replace at random with any number of little courtesies of your own choosing. Copy these. Laminate them. Put them up in the kitchen. You might as well use them as decoration. Because nothing will ever guarantee that you will be able to abide by them. And nothing can ensure that, even if you do, it'll all be fine. Our lives mostly tell us that the writers of fairy tales committed a huge cop-out when one of them hit on the idea of all stories ending, '. . . and they lived . . .'. Yeah, sure they did. Ever after. Anyone can write the bit leading up to that. But you have to decide to go one step further than Hans Christian Andersen to complete the next chapter where they're arguing about the gas bill, mopping baby sick up from the back of the car, or having an affair with the next-door neighbour, and make it a fun, romantic read. Life doesn't necessarily continue happily ever after, we know that. When a good joke survives it usually means there is a drop of truth in it. Remember the one about the ninety-year-old woman who went to the solicitors and asked him to get her a divorce? She said, 'I can't stand another moment with my husband.' The solicitor said, 'But you've been married for sixty-nine years. Why's it taken you till now?' And she replies, 'I wanted to wait until the kids had died.'

There is an advice mountain somewhere in the EU piled high with tips on dating, sex, love, divorce, separation, living together, living apart. You can find the perfect way to deal with any aspect you can imagine of the game of romance. And this advice is doled out as if you are a car in need of a service. Current culture has adapted Jane Austen: it is as if now the truth universally acknowledged is that a single person in possession of bad fortune in love must be in want of advice. You're just not doing it right, counsel the omnipresent experts both unsolicited and begged for. All you need to do is to pop into the emotional equivalent of Kwik-Fit and have your engine retuned and your exhaust adjusted and the course of love will run as smooth as silk. We are hopelessly prey to an idea of perfectability. Not to an idea that we are perfect. Much worse than that. That at least is an illusion that the mirror on your wall, or into your soul, can solve with a single glance. Much worse is the illusion that, knowing you are imperfect, you firmly believe that there is always something you can do about it. That you can fix it. That all you need is a little adjustment here or there. Pull this lever, nip this tuck, change this opinion, wear different shoes or, absurdly from one dating magazine, taste of vanilla. Yes! Taste! You can just choose from a million alterations suggested and you will bag your perfect man/woman/furry animal/Susan or Shaun. Because you know how to do it. You know the rules. And, like the Mounties, they will make sure you always get your man. Or woman.

Despite the ebbs and flows of permissions for certain kinds of behaviour, over history and in different cultures, the narrative of love has had some consistency in the Western tradition. But, still, whatever lessons there have been to learn, we haven't learnt them. We go on jousting at windmills, tripping over our hearts and telling the same stories. It makes me think of the inner ring road in Birmingham. Romance is a story driving round the historical equivalent of the Queensway. I don't know if you've ever done this, but you can drive for hours and hours circling the city centre never actually getting anywhere except where you've already been. You can't get off it. You get stuck on this road, which is at an odd level to the buildings. You can look over the edge and see the city both below and above you as you drive by. Birmingham seems to be the only city in Europe that has a mezzanine floor. And riding it reminds me of the endless repetitions of the trials of love.

Against this background there are the persistent questions that people bracket under the general title of manners and love. Whether or not you pay for dinner on a first date; how you ask someone at work to go for a meaningful drink; when is it fine to flirt; do you tell the truth on a first date; when do you suggest the first date; where do you go for it; when is it okay to suggest sleeping together; how you never ever ever ever stand anyone up; how do you dump someone when it's not working; how do you react as the dumpee and avoid throwing all their furniture out of the window and resist poisoning their pet? The dilemmas are backing up in a log jam on the inner city ring road. But in order to answer any of the questions – and remember that that assumes (a) we can, and (b) anyone in love or who's been dumped is ever likely to stick to any of the answers – we have to understand the forces buried deep in history that formed our conventions of love. We just don't behave as individuals. Rather, how we behave is to a large extent dictated by forces way beyond us which made a pretty good job at prescribing our roles. And the rules of the man: woman thing definitely spill over into the man:man or woman:woman thing. When we are in love we are in the grip of powerful cultural compulsions that have defined the rules. They have described romantic love, seduction, how we live under a tyranny of happy endings or terrible drudgery. And now, because we think we have greater choice, we have started to treat love as if it was another commodity to be consumed. Do you have that relationship in a smaller size, we seem to be asking. Have you got it in red? And, more and more, when relationships don't fulfil our own needs we just bugger off. It's a glorious freedom we have won. But we know there is a cost. How should our manners in love adapt?

For our purposes the story starts to be written down round about the year zero. There's certainly not so much that survives from way before that when a good date meant being dragged off by your hair into the nearest cave, tearing raw lion off the bone with your bare teeth as foreplay before making mad, passionate love on the sabre tooth tiger skin. Which, one way and another, is a bit too much raw animal for me. Despite what we can see in the drawings of beasts and symbols from some twenty thousand years ago that were discovered on cave walls in south-western France and around the Pyrenees and northern Spain, we can only speculate whether the original Flintstones were prepared for desire to steal valuable time away from sharpening their axes, hunting for prey and killing in order to eat, to have a rumble in the rubble. But certainly by the time Ovid wrote the *Amores* the seeds of romantic love had been sown. He published them in five books from about 20 BC. They were a kind of poetic part-work in which the hero is portrayed as enthralled by his love for a woman called Corinna. A slave to passion, the lover is shown sighing, trembling and even dying for love. The themes were all about amorous intrigue, which doesn't appear to have mirrored Ovid's own life terribly closely. Although he was married three times, two of them were very short and then the third lasted all the way through his exile until his death. And of that wife he apparently spoke very fondly.

But Ovid also collected and transformed into poetic shape a series of mythical stories in his most famous work, the *Metamorphoses*. In Book Four he tells the story of Pyramus and Thisbe, the founding tale of the star-crossed lovers, later the inspiration for Shakespeare's *Romeo and Juliet*. These are the original dippy, drippy teenagers in love that Marty Wilde was still wailing on about in the 1959 pop charts. You'll remember that they wanted to marry against their parents' wishes. The parents wouldn't relent, and presumably sent them to their separate bedrooms, whereupon they eloped. They agreed to meet under a mulberry tree in the forest. Poor little Thisbe arrived first, only to be scared away by the roar of a lion. But as she ran she dropped her veil. The lioness, presumably disappointed to have missed out on a tasty teenager, tore the veil to pieces instead. But she'd obviously eaten before because it got covered in ox blood. It wasn't – and this is not relevant to the chapter at all but may be worth pointing out – very good table manners to display greed so obviously. However, inevitably Pyramus showed up late, no doubt having got stuck with a mate listening to music, saw the blood and thought that his true love had been killed. So he did what any self-respecting teenager through history would have done. Instead of finding out where she'd gone, he made the loopiest and most irrational response to the situation. He instantly topped himself. Well, you would, wouldn't you? And then, of course, Thisbe came back. And she did what you can only do when you're a 'teenaaaaager in love'. She killed herself too.

Now I know there are tragic instances where this still actually happens, and I sincerely don't want to tread on anybody's grief. You have quite enough to deal with without me barging in. But short of literal suicide, every Adrian Mole, every Pandora, is still a latter-day Pyramus and Thisbe moping around their parents' house complaining that they will die if Tarquin or Miranda or Britney or Darren doesn't phone, text or e-mail within the next half an hour. It is the most important thing in their life. If the designated *amour* of the moment doesn't make contact their very existence will surely be challenged. They are on the utmost edge of an emotional crisis the size and scope of which their bloody parents can't possibly understand or relate to . . . man. They are, of course, practising for the grown-up version of this. The smitten lover. This was originally a man, but through a certain measure of equality has spread to women too. However, it developed its full cultural punch with men in the Middle Ages. Not their middle ages. Europe's.

In his later work *The Art of Love*, Ovid had ascribed to men in love symptoms as if they were ill. And they have dogged us ever since. Typical of a happily married man, he chose to visit on the rest of us poor singles a cultural sick-stick with which to beat our romantic backs. And with the help of the troubadours, the wandering minstrels of the eleventh century in southern France who, with their damned wandering, thus became the rats that carried the disease of romance all over Europe, he managed to infect us all with what became courtly love. To start with, to be in love you had to be unable to sleep, eat or drink and your health needed to fail. Feel familiar?

There were a whole set of other rules as well that emerged. For it to be courtly you had to be young and you fell in love with a woman who was married. This wasn't because she approved of adultery. It was to make her good and inaccessible. She was also, typically, older. It was a Mrs Robinson thing for the younger knights. They were practising and, in the literature although not in real life, she was in complete control. It was a falling in love with the boss's wife thing. Marriage for love, in Chaucer's *Franklin's Tale* for instance, was a radical idea. Marriages were for wealth, power and position. The young man's love for the lord's wife was a mirror to his relationship of fealty to the lord. All very feudal. The young man's adoration was also youthful randiness for an experienced woman, who at first would reject him and then play with his emotions. You can perm the combinations between men and women, to make it gay or straight. And you can even alter the age difference to make them equal. But it doesn't change the fact that what the troubadours set in motion was the pattern for the next thousand years of the hell and uncertainty of being in love. Oh, the exquisite pain of it all! (And if you're writing a teenage love diary, that exclamation mark has a circle with a frown in it at the bottom rather than a dot.)

By the time the troubadours had refined their songs and poems about love there was a pretty well-defined set of rules. Eleanor of Aquitaine, whose twelfth-century career was of such diplomatic unfeasibility that she managed to be both Queen of France and then of England, was a great fan of all courtly love. She did everything she could to encourage it through music and poetry. Her granddad William was said to have been one of the first troubadour poets and presumably wandered around with a lute doing all that moon, spoon in June nonsense. So with a hey nonny no, courtly love was eventually codified in a book in 1174 by Andreas Capellanus called, I think with admirable precision, *The Art of Courtly Love*. If you were to translate the elements he identified into the modern idiom – and who could resist – they might look like this:

You were smitten. It started with her beauty and then her face ate its way into your brain.

You couldn't tell her anything. Completely absurdly you had to keep it to yourself.

Then comes the not being able to eat, sleep or drink part.

Then you tell her. People don't write octosyllabic couplets as much as they used to but overemotional letters are what are required at this point. I love you. I cannot live without you. If you do not love me I will kill myself etc. Although as Tom Lehrer once cautioned, don't address them to 'Occupant'.

Even in the absence of a postal service you can't deliver them yourself. So you find a go-between. This is the wimple-era equivalent of 'my friend fancies you'.

The lady then pays no attention. She treats you to what that great inebriate Labour Chancellor George Brown called a complete ignoral.

Then she gives you a task. Earlier generations will remember it as a challenge of great derring-do to topple Jerusalem or kill a dragon. Those of you in your forties will perhaps better remember it through Monty Python's reluctant prince who was sent to the newsagent to get a packet of Rothmans.

Then, once the knight has completed the challenge, he wins the lady. But he still can't tell anyone. So they love through knowing glances and stolen moments.

She inspires him to do more than he ever dreamed he could and he becomes her champion.

Of course, they don't live happily ever after either because he gets fed up hanging around living only for the next doting yet furtive and celibate peek from his lady. And goes off with her daughter. Or they have a roll in the hay, are discovered and get banished by her husband the lord, to live in penury outside the kingdom. Which is not what either of them had in mind. She turns to drink and he to gambling. They get on each other's nerves. He starts to resent her age, she his youth. They brawl publicly in the tavern. And I think I am getting carried away now. None of Chaucer's stories quite ended like this.

The problem with this was that love was seen to

make men weak and the idealisation of women was little reflected in their real lives. They weren't treated any better because of their beauty, grace and all the other things the knights wrote and sang about. Rather their apparently magical powers over men probably made their situation worse. When Ibn Hazm wrote his treatise on love, *The Ring of the Dove*, he insisted that love was more transformative and balanced than this. It made the mean generous, the idiotic learned and the graceless gracious. He argued that love was not just the private inconsolable wailing of the unfulfilled but the greatest thing that could happen to two human beings. Which, of course, it is, if requited in equal measure and lasting. If it's not, then plan for a period of torture followed by depression, separation or divorce. He insisted that rather than using the language of love to mask who you were, love was that which truly revealed your identity. The language of love should be simple, clear and unambiguous. There was a difference between the sentimental moments of love, which tended towards it being a 'desirable sickness', and the search for self-knowledge. If the first problem with manners and love is that passion renders one's behaviour beyond control, then in the question of truth and love lies the second problem. Seduction.

Men and women seduce differently. Generally,

women seduce men by withholding sex, but not the possibility of it. Men seduce men by offering sex. As in, 'I'm not looking for Mr Right, I am looking for Mr Rightnow'. And to understand lesbians we need to turn to another joke – first told to me by my oldest lesbian friend, he says quickly by way of insurance. What does a lesbian bring on her second date? Answer: Everything. Lesbians seduce domestically with a cat basket and a catalogue. They don't offer sex; they offer a duvet and a damn good read. The great heterosexual female seducers in ancient legend are women like Cleopatra and Helen of Troy who both very successfully held out the possibilty of sex to capture powerful men. The central part of their story is that they lured the boys away from their toys with their beauty. The role of these woman was to try to get the man away from the public arena into the private, from the battlefield to the bedroom. That particular bit only worked to a limited extent in Helen's case. She married Menelaus but then ran away from him to Troy with the beautiful Paris. So the boys started a war. Not quite what she had envisaged. And it lasted ten years. But she did go back to her husband in the end and according to the legend . . . Yes, quite. They lived happily ever after.

Cleopatra's chosen method was to inveigle Julius Caesar on a trip down the Nile, which is still very reasonably priced, the travel agents tell us, if that takes your fancy and you need a man to restore your rule in your own kingdom. She set her cap at one of the most powerful men in the world for political reasons. Her voice, said Plutarch in his *Bioi Paralleloi* which, in an English version called *Parallel Lives*, was the basis for Shakespeare's Antony and Cleopatra, 'was like an instrument of many strings' and he went on to say that 'Plato admits four sorts of flattery, but she had a thousand'. She got exactly what she wanted from Caesar. She got to rule Egypt again. And she also got two weeks of constant sex, as the story goes, before he returned to Rome. Where he later built a gold statue to her.

The point of the way that women seduced men was that in order to get them to fall in love with them they had to entice them away from their usual territory of bashing each other over the head with weapons and wounding and killing each other. And into the boudoir. The modern equivalent of this battlefield is work. It's from worldly power that women are beckoning men. Because they'll never get some of them away from DIY or their motor. The myths had it that all these chaps who were possessed of the greatest temporal power in the world were, of course, reduced to little puppies and they were as putty in the hands of these siren seductresses. And the funny thing is that, however hard you try to parody this, however viciously you try to send it up or reduce it to silliness, it still contains the dreadful kernel of truth. Go to any pub on any Friday or Saturday night and there are the suburban Queens of Egypt dangling ostensibly big butch men on the strings of their withheld affection. The men may not all be senior management and powerful at work, but they try and give the impression of something close to being in charge of life. Although they don't look much like it when they are gazing metaphorically, if not actually, upwards with spaniel eyes at the woman of their desire hoping for some fruit to drop from the tree. For a bite of the apple. For a kiss before bedtime. Of course, there are variants. The confident women among you reading this, and the men who are happy with themselves now as fathers, nurturers and general all round wo-men, will protest. Things have changed and men and women don't behave like this any longer. Well, yes. There are variations of tone. You can sub-stitute the bohemian, new-man media atmosphere of the Groucho Club or the buttoned-up, chichi moneyed formality of the Savoy if you like. But underneath how much has it changed?

Men, on the other hand, mainly seduce women, and men, by lying. I don't mean that necessarily in a bad way. It's certainly not at all decent to fail to tell someone that you're married. In fact, let's be honest, it's sleazy. It dishonours everyone concerned. But that's at the far end of the mendacity spectrum. Though let's say you're single and free. On the first date, the first few dates, do you talk about the anxiety of work, money worries, your recent brush with rampant athlete's foot? Do you tell them when they have just said they think Julia Roberts is indeed worth $20 million a movie that you think she's a talentless wardrobe out of which she couldn't act her way? No, you don't. Is it good manners to lie? If you lie your way into a relationship, will you have to lie your way out?

The very epitome of the male seducer in legend was Don Juan. And the original play that was written about him in the early 1600s by a Spanish friar called Gabriel Tellez had the title *El Burlador de Sevilla*. Which sounds a lot more blunt if you don't speak Spanish. Translated he was reduced to *The Deceiver of Seville*. The play immortalised him as a liar. As he is warned in Act 1, 'By the same fate that you pretend to and deceive women, so will you pay with death.' But that didn't stop him. He lied his way into one bedroom after another. Or at least in the play four bedrooms and ever since a hell of a lot more. The first four belonged to women neatly divided across class and status: two noblewomen, Isabella and Dona Ana, and two so-called ordinary women, Tisbea and Aminta.

Don Juan embroidered the truth. The other great seducer, Casanova, embroidered what he wore. For a dandy like him, much of the art of seduction was about dressing up, metaphorically by not exactly telling the truth, and literally by dazzling the object of his desire with his clothes. He was a very natty looker. In one episode in his autobiography *Histoire de ma vie*, which told his life up to 1774 when he was almost fifty, he even went to a masked ball in Milan extravagantly dressed down. He created a costume to imitate a beggar in order to impress a woman he was after. It was a huge hit. Well, actually everything in his autobiography is a huge hit. He wrote it. And he was a terrible liar. A seducer, in fact. And so we learn on dates that truth serves us less well in prosecuting love than it does in a court of law. As Shakespeare said in Sonnet 138

> When my love swears that she is made of truth,
> I do believe her though I know she lies,
> That she might think me some untutored youth,
> Unlearned in the world's false subtleties.
> Thus vainly thinking that she thinks me young,
> Although she knows my days are past the best,
> Simply I credit her false speaking tongue,
> On both sides thus is simple truth suppressed:
> But wherefore says she not she is unjust?

And wherefore say not that I am old?
O loves best habit is in seeming trust,
And age in love, loves not t'have years told.
Therefore I lie with her, and she with me,
And in our faults by lies we flattered be.

It's a long way from the beauty and rhythm of Shakespeare's sonnet, but lying through appearance, rather than about our age, has reached a particular popular cultural peak recently with a TV series called *Queer Eye for a Straight Guy*. It starts with some dope from Bromley or Birmingham whose wardrobe comes entirely from Milletts Spring Collection. He is pounced on and stripped of his dullness by five homos from Soho like hyenas ripping the flesh from the carcass of an antelope. They go through his clothes, kitchen, bathroom, living room, music collection and anything else they can lay their manicured hands on. They try and turn him into a gay straight man in order to make him more appealing to women. And if that's not a lie then I'm Arnold Schwarzenegger.

Lying like this takes so many different forms, but it is one of the most enduring and essential tools of seduction. At the most extreme end in literature and occasionally in real life there are stories of what Shakespearean scholars call the 'bed-trick'. This involves going to bed with someone who you think you know and waking up and discovering it's in fact someone else. This is a whole stage further on from the old joke about how no one ever goes to bed with anyone ugly, but a lot of people wake up with someone who is. I used to describe it as the coyote moment. You wake up in the morning and look at them. And then you'd rather gnaw off your arm than wake them up. We all make mistakes based, of course, on the intoxicating combination, usually, of alcohol and lust. But you don't have to spend an afternoon in the Freud museum to realise that the myths which recount making love to someone whom you subsequently do not recognise speak of a very deep psychological unease. It happens in the Bible, the Arthurian legends, *All's Well That Ends Well* and *Measure for Measure*, the *Masquerades* of Boccaccio, *The Marriage of Figaro*, *Così fan Tutte*. The list is pretty long. It's all over literature. Often lovers simply trick their intended merely by the theatrical convention of putting on a mask.

It doesn't just appear in the classics either. Think of *Some Like It Hot*, *Tootsie*, *M. Butterfly*, *The Crying Game*, *Priscilla, Queen of the Desert*. None of these were quite art-house movies. They were Oscar-nominated popular successes. And each one had a love affair between a guy who was and a guy who turned out not to be. Which also, by the way, disproved the rather smart-aleck, but witty observation that the invention of the bedside light had made the bed trick rather more difficult to achieve than in Shakespeare's time.

In order to wonder productively whether it's fine to lie in love, you do have to ask just how true you are ever going to be in love. It's a very vexed question. There may be *veritas* in *vino*. But is there *veritas* in *coitu*? And should there be honesty in seduction? It's one of the most difficult axes of manners. We value the truth. But we also think we like politeness. In fact, we're damn sure we like politeness. But we also know that politeness involves not necessarily saying what we think or feel. Not always, but often it is a form of half-truth. And sometimes even lying. In it's most extreme form it's diplomacy, which Ambrose Bierce, who wrote the wonderful *Devil's Dictionary*, defined as 'n. Lying in state, or the patriotic art of lying for one's country'. Making sure someone else gets your way.

On the other hand we say we love honesty. Which we do. In Yorkshire they 'speak as they find' and we think they're marvellous for doing it. Until it's about us. When the truth gets a little too close to home, we think it's rather harsh and wish they had kept it to themselves. We have a similar ambivalence about harm. Try saying 'he or she is very charming' and at the same time thinking about different people you know who are. In the ones you trust, charm is a great virtue. You know you can rely on this person in any social situation. You can introduce them to your mother and be absolutely sure that they will come up dripping with her admiration. On the other hand, to the one you don't quite believe, the word charm is applied with a slight pause and there's a 'but' hanging around at the end of the sentence. There's almost a sneer in your tone and a definite question mark. We know that charming is thus applied to grace and comfort as much as it is to distrust and unease. Charm is the greatest gift a seducer can have. Worryingly, it may be precisely because you almost can't trust it. And it works. You only have to watch a charmer in action, as if they have eyes for no one else.

You can try this yourself. All you need to know is that, according to Harvard psychologist Zick Rubin in an article called 'Measurement of Romantic Love', published in the *Journal of Personality and Social Psychology*, couples in love supposedly look at each other for about 75 per cent of the time. I've always thought it was anxiety, but apparently it's love. The rest of us spend anywhere between 30 and 60 per cent of the time in eye contact. Well, there is some evidence to suggest that when we are in love we release a chemical cousin to amphetamine called phenyl ethylamine (PEA). This is supposedly what makes your palms sweat and your tummy go funny. There are suggestions in several dating manuals that you can deliberately make this happen. You can trick the brain of the man or woman you want to seduce by looking at him or her for 75 per cent of the time. I know staring is rude, but give it a go because it isn't in this case. By doing this you can provoke the release of PEA and make them fall for you. Now don't try this at home. It's dangerous. You may fall in love with your partner again. And it may only be partly true. But it's the same kind of trick as lowering the lights. There have been many experiments that have shown that men and women are more attracted to men and women whose pupils are enlarged. I don't want to use the phrase 'puppy eyes', because I don't want us to experience any throwback to teenage crushes on Donny Osmond and feel overhumiliated by this. But again you can trick someone with the big toffee-eye look. Just lower the lights. Your pupils will naturally widen. And then, of course, they will fall for you and live with you for the rest of your natural life. Which, if they're superficial enough to fall for you just because you've got big pupils, may turn out to be a bit of a trial.

All of this may not be a good idea if we want to live a world of total truth. But if you want to draw the person of your dreams – who may, of course, still turn out to be the one of your nightmares – further along the path of romance, you could give it a go. And be honest: do you want to be told the truth all the time in love? God forbid. I don't want to be wooed by the man who does little else but point out my faults and list his own. Do you? Is real love only ever based on truth? We talk about the mystery of love. Well, it fades. But don't let it fade too soon. Certainly not on the first date. And don't let manners be adduced in the case for the prosecution of the use of lies in flirtation.

Falling in love is a frightening business. It's full of the possibility of hurt. When you have set your heart on someone, to find they have not set their heart on you makes you feel idiotic. As if you've shown something private, embarrassing, to the wrong person. Despite the fact that everyone you know has experienced this too, it still feels as if you have slipped on the most obvious of life's banana skins. It's as if the whole world is for the moment laughing at you because, as the song goes, you are a fool. Manners have their role to play in this. The conventions of love help you to fall gracefully. Who needs help when you're flying on the wings of reciprocated desire? Sail aloft and just be careful, unlike Icarus, not to soar too close to the sun and crash to earth. It's when it goes wrong we need help. Or when we are beset by such uncertainty that we dare not dare. In all cases of love what we need is a gentle takeoff and landing. Manners can help. The rules of courtly love may look silly and effete, but at least they codified the steps of romance. Chaucer said that 'love is blynde'. The conventions of the Middle Ages were a braille map through the process of infatuation. They were probably not rules for real life. Scholars have argued about whether they were to be understood literally or merely a kind of courtly game played out through literary means. There are stories from the court of Eleanor of Aquitaine of trials under the code of courtly love, but they were probably no more than hypothetical cases of how love should be pursued. Because with love rules are almost always an aspiration.

To make things worse in all this we are drugged on happy endings. We dream of everything going right. We are addicted to the moment when Snow White is woken by the Prince's kiss. Or vice versa. For Prince here read Princess. For male, female. Because men and women, gay and straight, are all similarly prey to the tender trap of romance, even if we don't wholly believe it or admit it. And the difficulty is not how to handle the passion, but how to rescue our feelings from the pile-up. We can handle the fantasy, the honeymoon. But when an affair tumbles from the sky, the black box is endlessly examined with friends. And questions are asked. Who behaved badly? Well, of course, the one who isn't your friend. And who behaved well? Well, of course, your friend. Was the dumper or the romantic refusnik well mannered about it? Inevitably no. Let's face it, there is no easy way to tell someone that you don't love them, that you don't fancy them. And even more so, there are few graceful ways to tell someone that you don't love them any longer. To do it and still be thought honourable is the height of good manners.

But there are certainly fewer conventions now than there were at the start of the last century. Which is not bad but it's confusing. The balance between men and women had to change. When Emmeline Pankhurst and the Women's Social and Political Union started to chain themselves to railings and throw themselves under the King's horse, the bonds of wifely servitude were rightly beginning to be tested. The difficulty for us with relationships and manners is that manners are at their best when there are maxims to obey. That's what makes them manners. But the best you can say about Victorian marriage was that in prison at least you knew the rules. And they were unconscionable. The husband was lord and master and the wife his submissive prop. No argument about that. It may have worked for one woman in a million. It was a living hell for most of them. But there were no demarcation disputes between what was required of men and of women. I'm not arguing for it. Don't hold me to that. I'm just making the point that in this situation, while humanity was tested to the limits of endurance and personal freedom was sacrificed, there was a clear set of axioms to be obeyed.

When women rebelled, it led towards emancipation. Through the great struggles of women who struck, worked to rule, campaigned and fought those who would set them back, women and men all veered towards some messy, very sketchy but nonetheless wonderful approximation to equality. And it's thrown everyone into total confusion. Because people don't think they know how to behave in love any more.

In advanced capitalist societies, the balance has shifted not just between men and women but also between the traditional and the individual. We are cast adrift on a sea of personal emotions and it causes us anxiety. We have freedom but a great deal less certainty. And we are far more likely to think of our personal relationships as exactly that. They are all about our own personal development, our own needs so when a relationship stops fulfilling those we feel less troubled about chucking it out and getting a newer mode.

I got dumped recently. By text. And more of that in a while. The person concerned ditched me despite thinking he 'was passionately in love' with me on the Wednesday before the Monday. And there'll be no more said about that. Because the point here is he chucked me because he 'needed a boyfriend in London'. That's it. Exactly. I know, of course, because, like every actor who's ever forgotten their lines even once is still able recite with complete recall their bad reviews I, like all of you, will be able to remember for the rest of my life the exact words with which I was junked. I am afraid – no I am not, I am filled with the holy pleasure of having delivered a good put-down exactly when it was needed and not three days later – that I immediately replied, by text naturally, that he must have gone to the wrong section of the boyfriend department store when he acquired me since my label clearly said 'Brighton'. He'd been window shopping but clearly bought the wrong gift. This, in a variety of forms, is how we now conduct relationships. And in many ways it's great. How many times do we need to emphasise to ourselves the sheer degree of liberty, which has flown as much from the great leap of contraceptive freedom as it did from the politics of equality developed by the Victorian and Edwardian women struggling out of domestic slavery? But, equally, 'pure love' relationships, as they're known in the post-modern political science trade, barter freedom for uncertainty.

If tradition no longer informs our relationships as much as it did, and they are more about us as individuals now than they are about the context of our traditions and culture, then they are guided by personal choice. And more often than not that is abetted by experts, either the self-appointed emotional gurus of magazines and TV, or just the friends that surround us. We go to therapy rather than our parents for support, to our friends rather than our grandparents for advice. Yet – and here we come back to where we started – the group of the romantic traditions is still surprisingly strong. There is a sense out there that we are still loving, and wanting to love, in quite a traditional way.

Talking to people in the street recently for a television piece about all of this, one moment stood out. I had thrust the microphone under the noses of middle-aged, old-aged, young, black, white, Chinese, Scandinavian, Australian men and women, on their own, in couples of all sorts, arm in arm as obvious lovers and in any number of combinations of friends and family. Slightly to my surprise they had all revealed a remarkable degree of consistency in wanting some conventions. I began to wonder if I was just asking very square people. Then appeared this young woman. Maybe twenty-one or two. She would never have made it through a metal detector and got on a plane. She was a walking hardware store. A silver peacock, she was pierced from crest to toe. And she looked like she had the plots of the novels of Terry Pratchett tattooed on her body. Young, independent, an upright bed of nails, she was magnificently rebellious. And her language matched. 'Can I ask you a question?' 'Yeah,' she sneered a sexy smile. 'Do you date boys or girls?' 'Boys.' 'Well then, if you went to eat somewhere on a first date, would you expect him to pay?' 'Course I fucking would. Cos he's a fucking bloke.' 'Would you worry that that might mean he'd expect you to sleep with him?' 'Course I fucking would because he's a fucking bloke.' Then she added, 'But I wouldn't.' Traditional values in a modern setting!

We still need some rules. They need to encompass independence and equality. We need to make some decisions now to root us again in some context approaching certainty. So, both daft and serious, these are some modest modern suggestions for the twenty-first century.

MEETING, FLIRTING, DATING AND LOVING

You dancing? You asking? I'm asking. I'm dancing. One way and another that's how it's supposed to go.

Eyes meet across a crowded club or bar and $e=mc^2$. In fact, most people meet through friends. So rule number one. It's good manners to match-make. Introduce your friends to each other. Hardly anyone kisses the boy next door any more. It's not that he's short of snogs, it's just that he probably comes from further afield. In cultures where marriages are not arranged, we are more likely to fall for the girl over dinner, the boy with mates in the pub, the wholly unsuitable young man with the slim hips, the beautiful smile and loads of potential if he can just get through college who came to the bar that night with your friend. Maybe the last one is just me. If manners are about our ability to get on, and in this case maybe get off, with each other, then we need the environment in which to meet. We are more atomised than we have ever been before in a society that is less rooted in geography. Manners are about creating the atmosphere in which we can flourish socially with each other. They lubricate social intercourse. It's hard to talk to a stranger. And it's hard to trust a stranger who talks to you. Strangers are wary of each other. So don't just sit there like a lump. Stop imitating vegetation. Introductions matter. Make an effort. We are less formal than we used to be so we have to invent new conventions. We all rely on friends to go over and inform some luckless boy or girl 'my friend fancies you'. We should do this more. It allows for both a graceful refusal or an enthusiastic yippee. At parties, rather than bars, it's much easier to walk straight up to complete strangers and say hello. The chances are you'll have to start with something that, in retrospect, will seem monumentally dull. Either that or you'll be so nervous you'll chuck your drink over them by accident. At least that'll start something. Hell, speaking to someone for the first time is nightmarish, so friends should help as much as possible.

Especially since there's less work done with fans these days, which one might think is a matter for regret. How much more fun than standing, stuttering in front of the object of your desire would it be to use one of the thirty-three ways to hold a fan listed in a book translated into English, rather inevitably from the Spanish, by Duvelleroy of Paris in the mid-eighteenth century. You could signal being 'desirous of acquaintance' by holding it with the left hand in front of your face, 'you are too willing' by carrying it in your right hand. To snarl, 'I hate you', simply draw it through the hand. More poignantly, to say, 'I love another', you could twirl it in the right hand; to say, 'I love you', draw it across your cheek (which, it doesn't specify); and, finally, to promise marriage you shut the fully opened fan, very slowly. And all the while you can pretend to be Glenn Close and John Malkovich.

It's not entirely easy to see how this kind of demented semaphore might achieve the object of discretion, but I guess it beats standing looking like the saddo at the end of the bar trying to smile at someone you think you like.

The modern equivalent of fanwork must be texting; the sheer joy of text as a flirting tool is unbounded. It allows almost total freedom. Just don't persist if they don't respond. You won't be able to see that but they'll be holding their phone in their right hand.

In the absence of fans, and even if you're texting desirously, there needs to be a dance of discovery. So flirt. We have already used history to give us permission to tell little lies. Not big ones. They dishonour. But if you are meeting for the first time, manners require that both of you create some space in which neither of you is yet to feel awkward, to be nailed to the definite. Although you may find that for you the biggest sexual charge comes from direct confrontation. In which case, seconds out of the ring. Two of my greatest friends, soul mates and now married, argued so badly on their first meeting that she left the table and went for a walk on the beach. They are now blissful. But just to align metaphor and reality, they really should have got married on 5 November, Bastille Day or . . . you get the point?

They understood each other immediately. The

graceful way to discover how you feel about each other is to read the evidence. If you are truly wild for them, you will, of course, ignore negative clues completely. But do try not to. There are two questions you never need to ask in life. Do you fancy me and are you famous? You will know the answers to both without asking, the first by instinct and the second by logic. If you don't know them, they aren't. Oh, and I should add, 'Do you love me?' That is the most dangerous question that is ever asked. And you can't pretend you haven't asked it by telling them that you love them. When you tell someone that you love them, it's frequently a sentence with a question mark at the end of it. In love we need the manners to protect our hearts a little. Even though we know that we won't.

However, I found on the University of Houston's Digital History site an intriguing story of seduction, if this can truly be called that, by truth. In the mid-1830s in America a well-known abolitionist called Theodore Dwight Weld, who in 1833 was one of the founders of the American Anti-Slavery Society, married Angelina Grimke, the daughter of a wealthy slaveholding family from South Carolina who had subsequently turned against slavery. They spent the whole of their courtship listing their personal faults, from selfishness and pride to the fact that she had once loved another man and he was a rather sloppy dresser. They thought it wrong to marry until they knew everything about each other. And in the end they did get married, proving once again that there is less correlation than one might wish for between the nobility of the cause that people support and the amount of fun they are at a party. Honesty will fulfil its role when a relationship is real. But play a little before that.

There are a few things people always want to know:

- Men and women are equally capable of asking each other out on a date.
- Men, when they are on a date with a woman, have always paid for dinner. Surely now history has brought us to a place of albeit approximate equality and emancipation, isn't it best that if one of you can, then do. And the other person, man or woman, pay for something else – champagne, movie tickets. Treat each other. And if you can't afford to do that, go Dutch and pretend that you're paying for each other. And now that the closet door has swung wide open, and the love that dares not speak its name has developed a rather lovely speaking voice, these matters are slightly complicated by the difficulty of differentiation, as I once heard it described in a stuffy sociology

lecture. Who pays if both of you are guys? Or women? The same rules apply – treat each other.

- Chairs should only be held for people who will appreciate it.
- If someone wants to sleep with you, you will know. Don't beg. We all have. We all will again. But it's embarrassing when you wake in the morning alone and the terrible memory of what you did comes flooding back and the bed whistles with the icy draft of humiliation.
- If you don't fancy someone, be gentle. We all appreciate it when it happens to us. And don't tell them you think they're really nice . . . God, that gets up my nose. I know it's an attempt to be decent, but when what you want is sex, it is no help at all to be told that you're really interesting or you've got the biggest brain on the planet. At that point you want to be Julia Roberts or Tom Cruise. Not Stephen Hawkins.
- Don't kiss like a sink plunger. It's rude. If manners are about negotiating our social relationships, then explore. Don't do invasive surgery. Kissing should be gradual, each seeking permission. Unless, of course, it's an immediate mutual tonsillectomy. But manners require you to make sure that it is and not to assume.
- If you fancy someone and they give you their

phone number, when do you ring them for a date? Personally, I have premature communication. I can't resist doing it immediately. But then you run the risk of them holding their fan in their right hand. You should wait a day. And that doesn't include the day you got the number. So there's that day plus the next day. And then you can call after that. So that's Monday after the Saturday, for those of you with mental arithmetic deficits. You won't wait that long, of course. But you asked and that's industry standard. But then there are the tantric flirters. They extend the process to Buddhist lengths. They don't ring for weeks.

- Never dump anyone by text. It's really cowardly. But more than that the purpose of manners is social cohesion. Being let go, as they say in industry – and for men it sure has the ability to downsize – is quite simply the pits. It's horrible. It provokes anger, sadness and great feelings of self-hatred. It always amazes me that when they get the push so many people crumble into self-blame. It's like, Hey, why bother feeling angry with them when one can lie on the floor of one's life and develop the emotional equivalent of eczema. Go on, turn it in on yourself! When you decide to leave someone you are in the strongest position, no matter how bad you may feel about it. Manners dictate that you treat them with respect. You have to do it in person, you have to listen to them and you may not have to tell them the whole truth. It's obviously different if you've only been together for a short while than if you've been together for years. Be gentle either way.

- There is nothing in any of the above, which means that if you meet through the internet you behave with any less respect towards people. The degree of anonymity given by technology, the distances that it can enable you to cross, do not absolve any of us from the demands of manners. It's just another way of meeting. Speed dating, internet dating, dating agencies: they are all just technological versions of the old Jewish matchmaker. If you think the internet is pretty neat when you're surfing for girls or boys just remember that, breathtaking a technology as it may be, underneath it's just Barbra Streisand in *Hello Dolly*.

- If you make a date, stick to it. There are only two reasons not to show. A death in the family and the last episode ever of *Friends* is on and the video, DVD recorder, TiVo and Sky Plus are all on the blink, your mobile phone doesn't work and evil spirits came in through the window and kidnapped you and took you to an alien planet and you cannot communicate with anyone one in the earth's galaxy . . . You get the idea. What could be worse manners than to invite another human being to eat, to drink, to share with you? And not to show up. It doesn't have to be said, does it? Apparently sometimes it does.

- Manners makes one clear rule about all of this – never force anything on anyone. Apparently that still needs saying too.

—✐—

POSTSCRIPT

This journey through manners has left me, and I sincerely hope you too, with a spirit of optimism rather than depression. It is more stoical than skipping lightly through the fields. There's a sort of *nil bastardum carborundum* feel to the campaign now, as my maths teacher used to put it in his pidgin Latin: don't let the bastards grind you down. But there is a great sense among so many of us that we know what manners are. We know that it comes down to a very simple principle: think not just of yourself but of others. Treat people in the way you would like to be treated. We have discovered that even though we must be prepared to banish the selfishness that recent generations seem to have learnt, this means not harking back, but rather establishing a new sense of respect for each other in a different and changed world. In *The Age of Extremes*, Eric Hobsbawm organised what he called the short twentieth century into an Age of Catastrophe, from 1914 to the end of the Second World War, a brief Golden Age of prosperity and growth until the 1970s, which then transformed in the last part of the century into 'an era of decomposition, uncertainty and crisis'. We are reordering that crisis. There is a palpable sense among us that we want authority that we can respect, behaviour we can admire and rules that we can follow willingly without the coercion of violence or oppression. Our desire for true manners is a sign of that. Our confidence to create a sense of shame in those who trespass on our desire to live at ease with each other is growing. Now is the time to make it heard. Now is the time for our campaign of civil obedience to take flight. That is, if you wouldn't mind awfully joining in.

—∽∽—

BIBLIOGRAPHY

Brewer, John, *The Pleasures of the Imagination*, London: HarperCollins, 1997

Collins, Marcus, *Modern Love*, London: Atlantic Books, 2003

Delaney, Carol, *Investigating Culture*, Oxford: Blackwell, 2004

Donkin, Richard, *Blood, Sweat & Tears*, New York and London: Textere, 2001

Elias, Norbert, *The Civilizing Process*, Oxford: Blackwell, 1994

Encyclopaedia Britannica, Standard Edition, 2004 (CD-ROM)

Erasmus, 'De Civilitate Morum Puerilium' ('On Good Manners for Boys'), trans. Brian McGregor, in Vol. 25, 'Collected Works of Erasmus: Literary and Educational Writings 3'; ed J. Kelly Sowards,

University of Toronto Press, 1985, pp. 269–289. Reprinted with kind permission.

Fox, Kate, *Watching the English*, London: Hodder & Stoughton, 2004

Fox, Valentine, *I Can See Your Lips Moving*, Essex: Plato Publishing, 1993

Haiman, John, *Talk is Cheap*, Oxford: Oxford University Press, 1998

Hobsbawm, Eric, and Ranger, Terence, eds, *The Invention of Tradition*, Cambridge: Cambridge University Press, 1983

Hunt, Tristram, *Building Jerusalem*, London: Weidenfeld & Nicolson, 2004

Isaacs, William, *Dialogue*, New York: Currency Doubleday, 1999

Langford, Paul, *A Polite and Commercial People*, Oxford: Clarendon Press, 1989

Lincoln, Abraham, *The Collected Works of Abraham Lincoln*, Illinois: The Abraham Lincoln Association, 1953. Reprinted with kind permission of the State of Illinois.

McCrum, Robert, MacNeil, Robert, and Cran, William, *The Story of English*, London: Faber & Faber, 2002

Martin, Judith, *Miss Manners' Guide for the Turn-of-the-Millennium*, New York: Fireside Books/Simon & Schuster, 1990

Miller, Samantha, *E-Mail Etiquette*, New York: AOL Time Warner, 2001

Mitford, Nancy, *Noblesse Oblige*, Oxford: Oxford

University Press, 2002

Morgan, John, *Debrett's New Guide to Etiquette and Modern Manners*, New York: St Martin's Press, 1996, reprinted by permission of Hodder Headline Limited

Parris, Matthew, *Scorn*, London: Hamish Hamilton, 1994

Post, Emily, *Etiquette* (17th edn), New York: HarperCollins, 2004

Pring, Adele, *Astronomy and Australian Indigenous People*, Aboriginal and Cultural Studies and Reconciliation, Aboriginal Education Unit, Government of South Australia, 2002

Putnam, Robert, *Bowling Alone*, New York: Simon & Schuster, 2000

Ridley, Matt, *The Origins of Virtue*, London: Penguin, 1997

Sennett, Richard, *The Corrosion of Character*, New York: W. W. Norton, 1998

Shakespeare, William, *The Sonnets of William Shakespeare*, London: Shepheard-Walwyn, 1974

Visser, Margaret, *The Rituals of Dinner*, London: Penguin, 1991

Walker, John, ed., *Halliwell's Filmgoer's Companion* (10th edn), London: HarperCollins, 1993

Zeldin, Theodore, *An Intimate History of Humanity*, London: Vintage, 1998

Zhou Nan-Zhao and Teasdale, Bob, eds, *Teaching Asia-Pacific Core Values of Peace and Harmony: A Sourcebook for Teachers*, Bangkok: UNESCO, 2004

USEFUL WEB SITES

About.com
http://www.weddings.about.com/cs/justforfun/a/Short-
  CelebWeds.htm
Digital History
http://www.digitalhistory.uh.edu
Edward Alexander Westermarck
http://www.kirjasto.sci.fi/ewester.htm
The Funeral Directory.com
http://www.thefuneraldirectory.com/ancientrites.html
Gaskell's Compendium (Letters of Condolence)
http://www.people.virginia.edu/~rmf8a/gaskell/
Gateway Ukraine
http://www.brama.com/

Interpretive Resources
Luther & Philip of Hesse
http://www.newadvent.org/cathen/09438b.htm
Matrimonials India
http://www.matrimonialsindia.com/index.htm
Marriage in USA
http://www.marriageequalityca.org/history_marriage.
   php
Office of National Statistics (marriage)
http://www.2-in-2-1.co.uk/ukstats.html
http://www.statistics.gov.uk/CCI/nugget.asp?ID=432
Republic of Pemberley
http://www.pemberley.com/
Joseph Schumpeter
http://www.transcriptions.english.ucsb.edu/archive/
   courses/liu/english25/materials/schumpeter.html
Sneezing
   http://www.netlaputa.ne.jp/~tokyo3/e/sneeze_e.html
Teaching Asia-Pacific Core Values of Peace and
   Harmony: A Sourcebook for Teachers Chapter Six
   Cultural Values of Peace in the Pacific Islands: A
   Case Study of Samoa Penelope S. Meleisea,
   Antropologist, University of Auckland
http://www.unescobkk.org/ips/ebooks/documents/sou
   rcebook_teachers/
Wedding Rituals
http://www.factmonster.com/ipka/A0767684.html

Wedding Guide.com
http://www.weddingguide.co.uk/
Work Foundation
http://www.theworkfoundation.com/research/
   publications.jsp

INDEX